COLOR
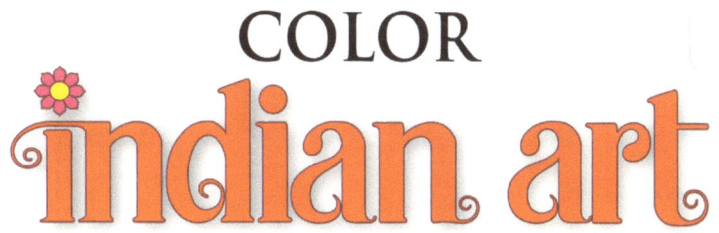
indian art

Conceived, Designed, and Illustrated by:

Mrinal Mitra

Series Edited by:

Swarna Mitra & **Malika Mitra**

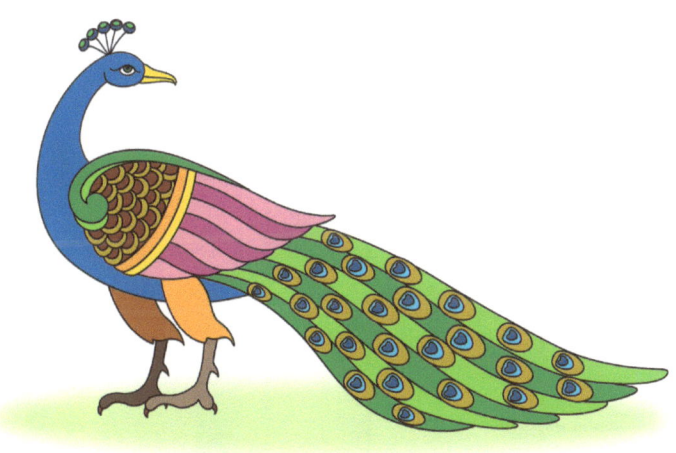

WORLD CULTURE COLORING SERIES

This series is dedicated to the citizens of the world;
from the young blooming minds of children, to the aspired individuals of all ages.

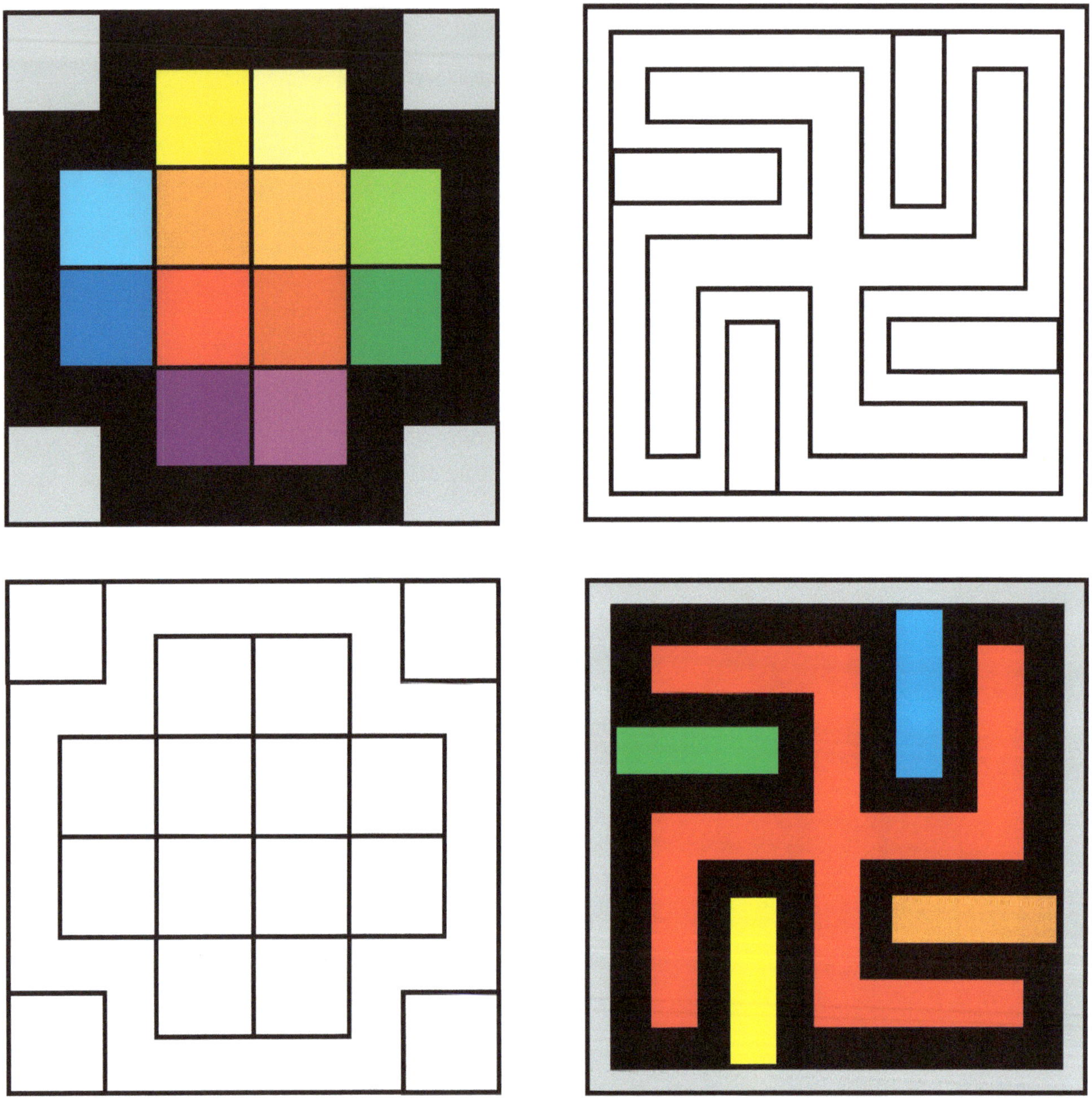

Multiple Cross, and Swastika. On seals found at Mohenjo-Daro, in the Harappan Civilization. 5000 years ago.

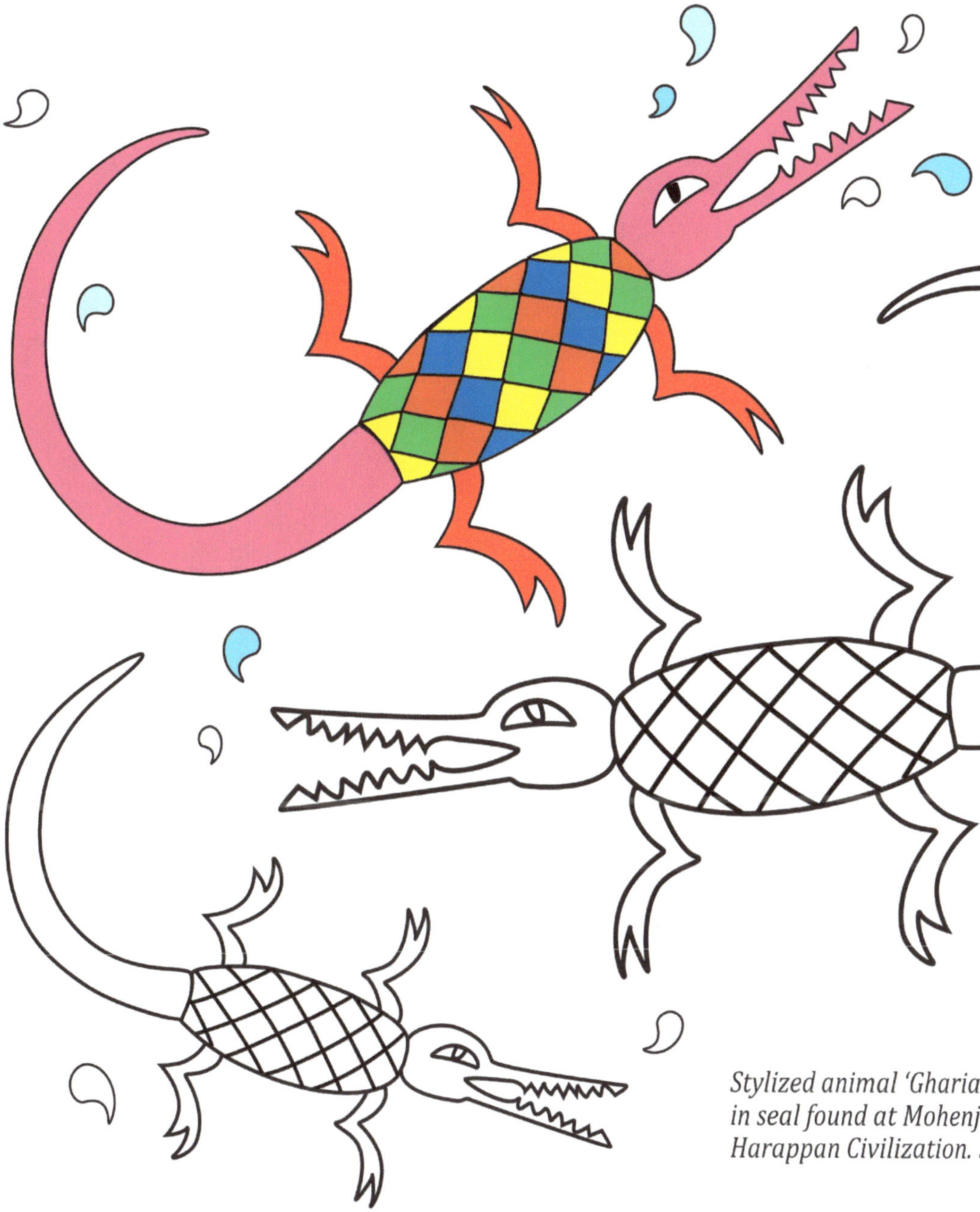

Stylized animal 'Gharial' engraved in seal found at Mohenjo-Daro in the Harappan Civilization. 5000 years ago.

Color the drawings above using your preferred choice of colors.

3

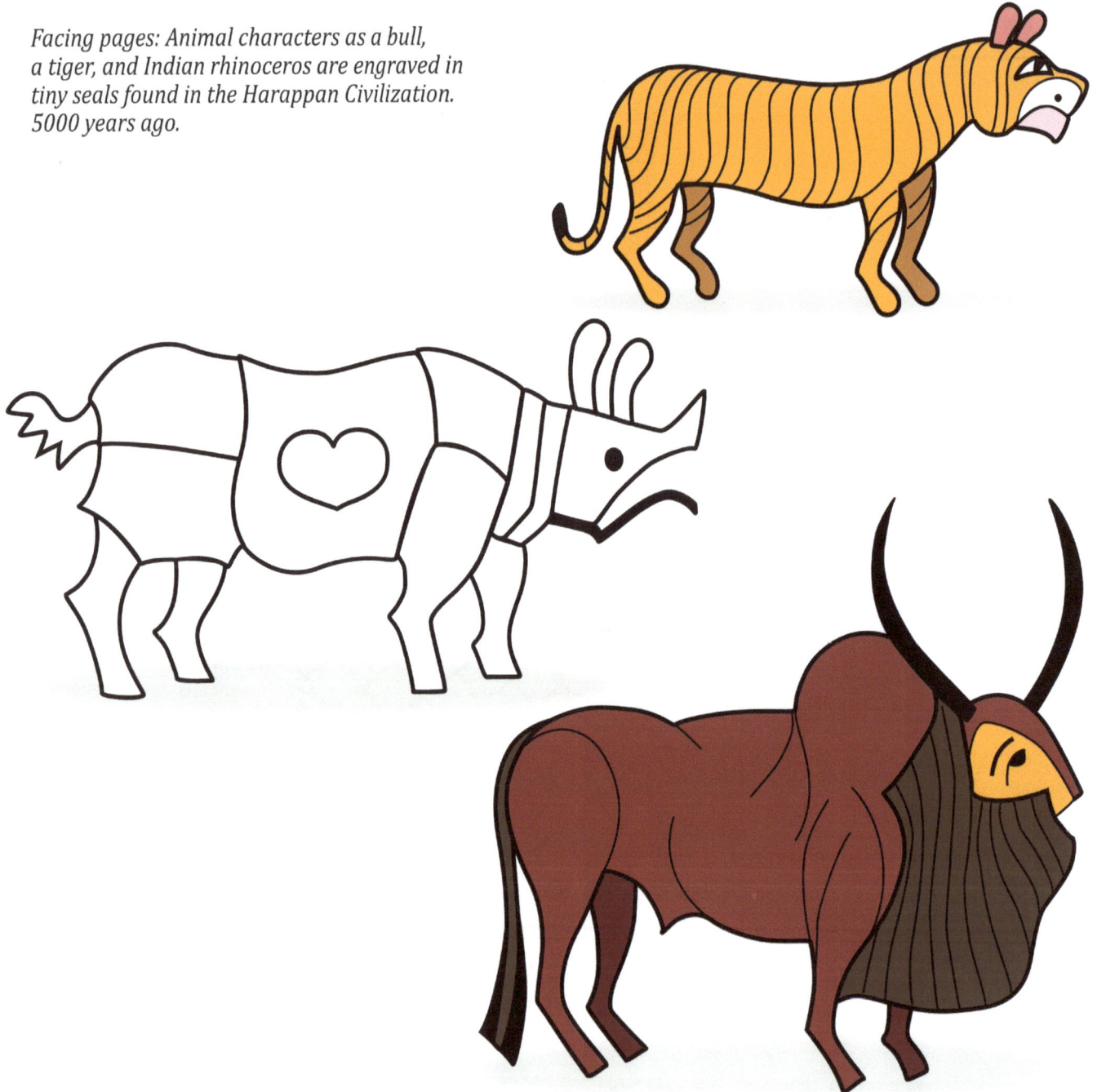

Facing pages: Animal characters as a bull, a tiger, and Indian rhinoceros are engraved in tiny seals found in the Harappan Civilization. 5000 years ago.

Color the drawings above using your preferred choice of colors.

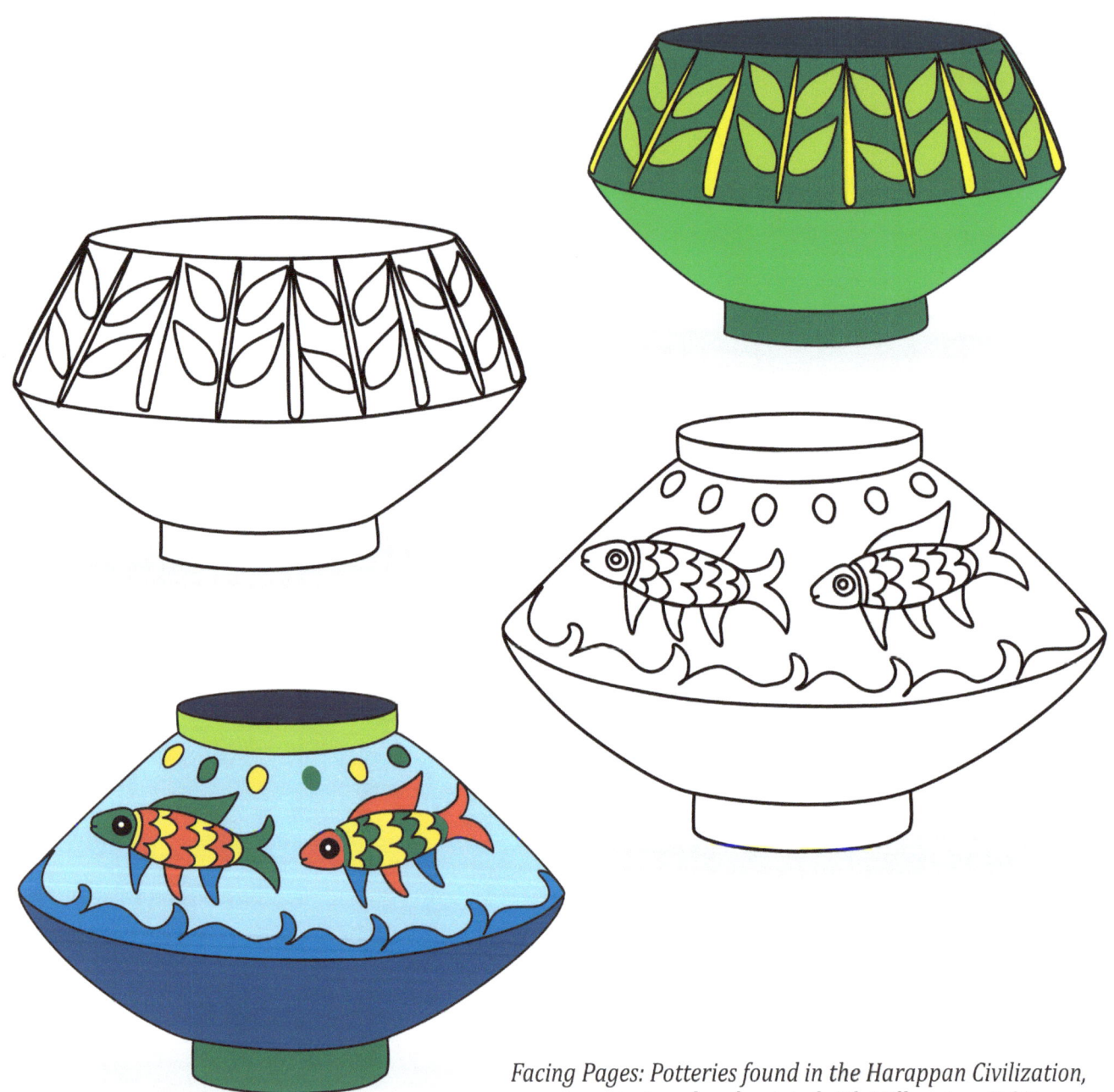

Facing Pages: Potteries found in the Harappan Civilization, were textured and painted. 4th Millennium B.C.E.

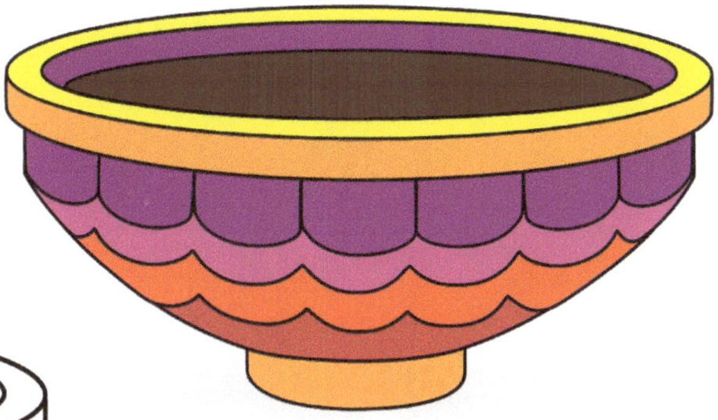

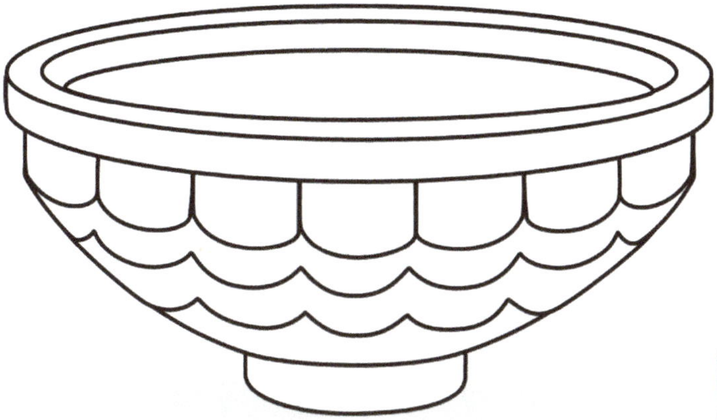

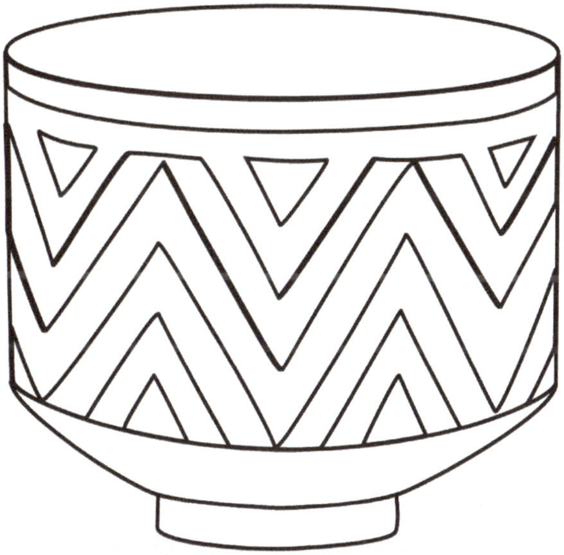

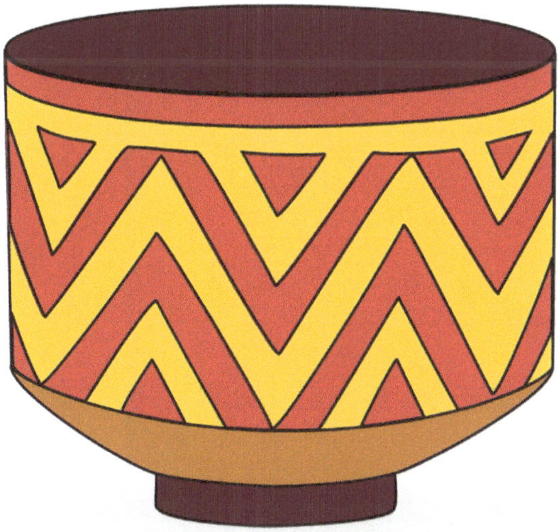

Color the drawings above using your preferred choice of colors.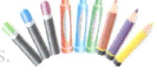

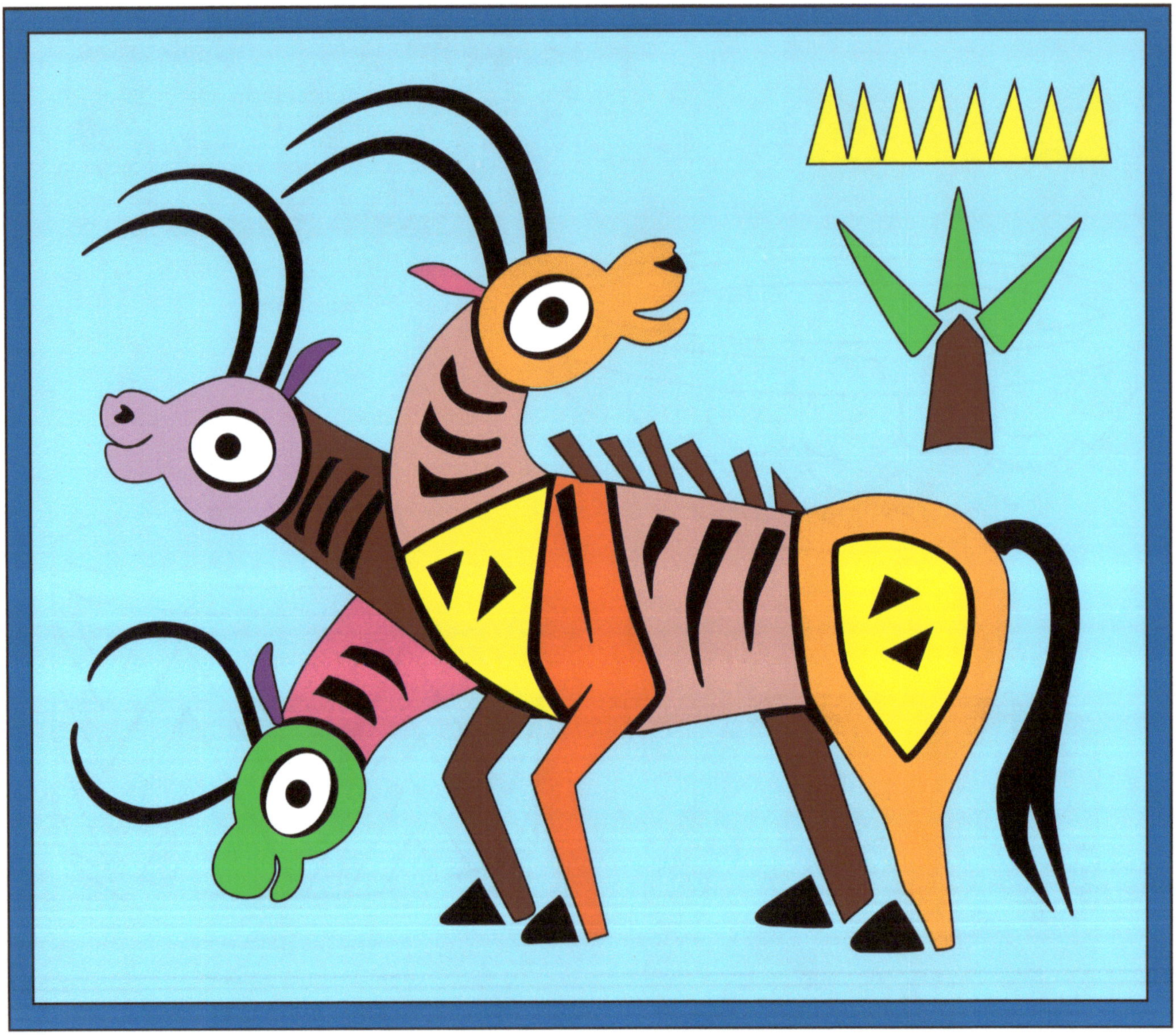

On seals found at Mohenjo-Daro, in the Harappan Civilization.
Depicting the strange animal. 5000 years ago.

8

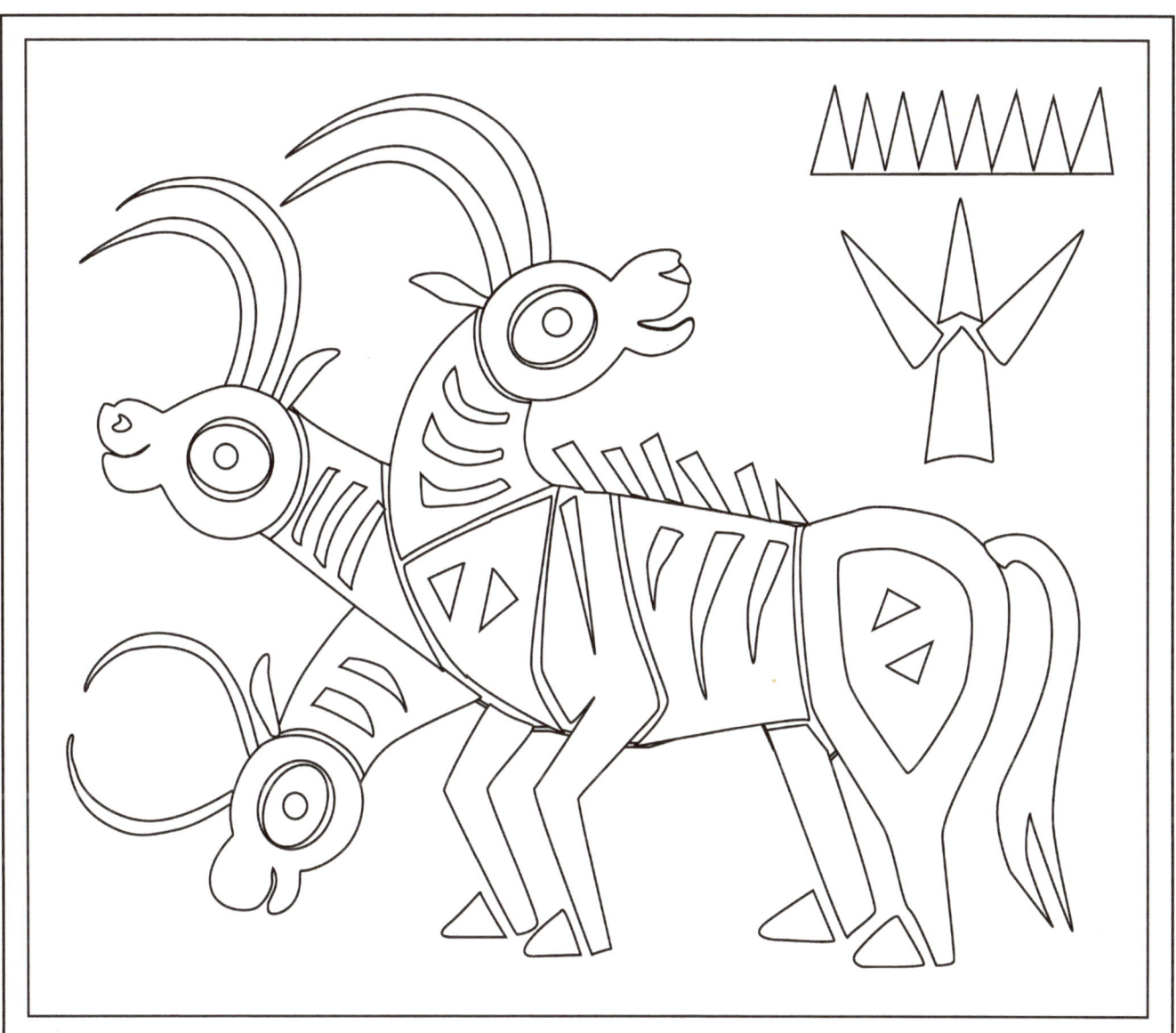

Color the drawing above using your preferred choice of colors.

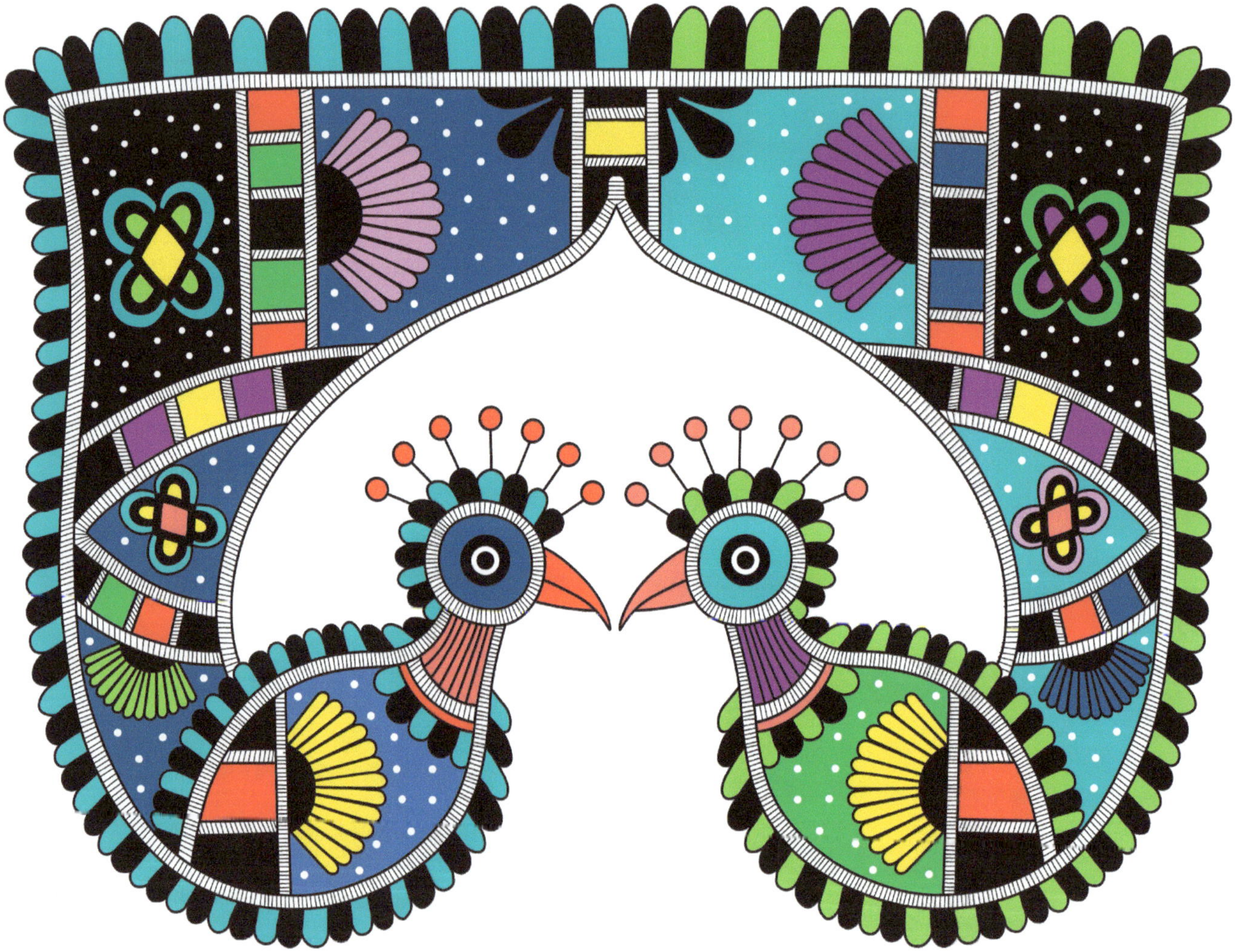

Two peacocks. The peacock is a symbol of eternity in Mithila paintings. Bihar, India.

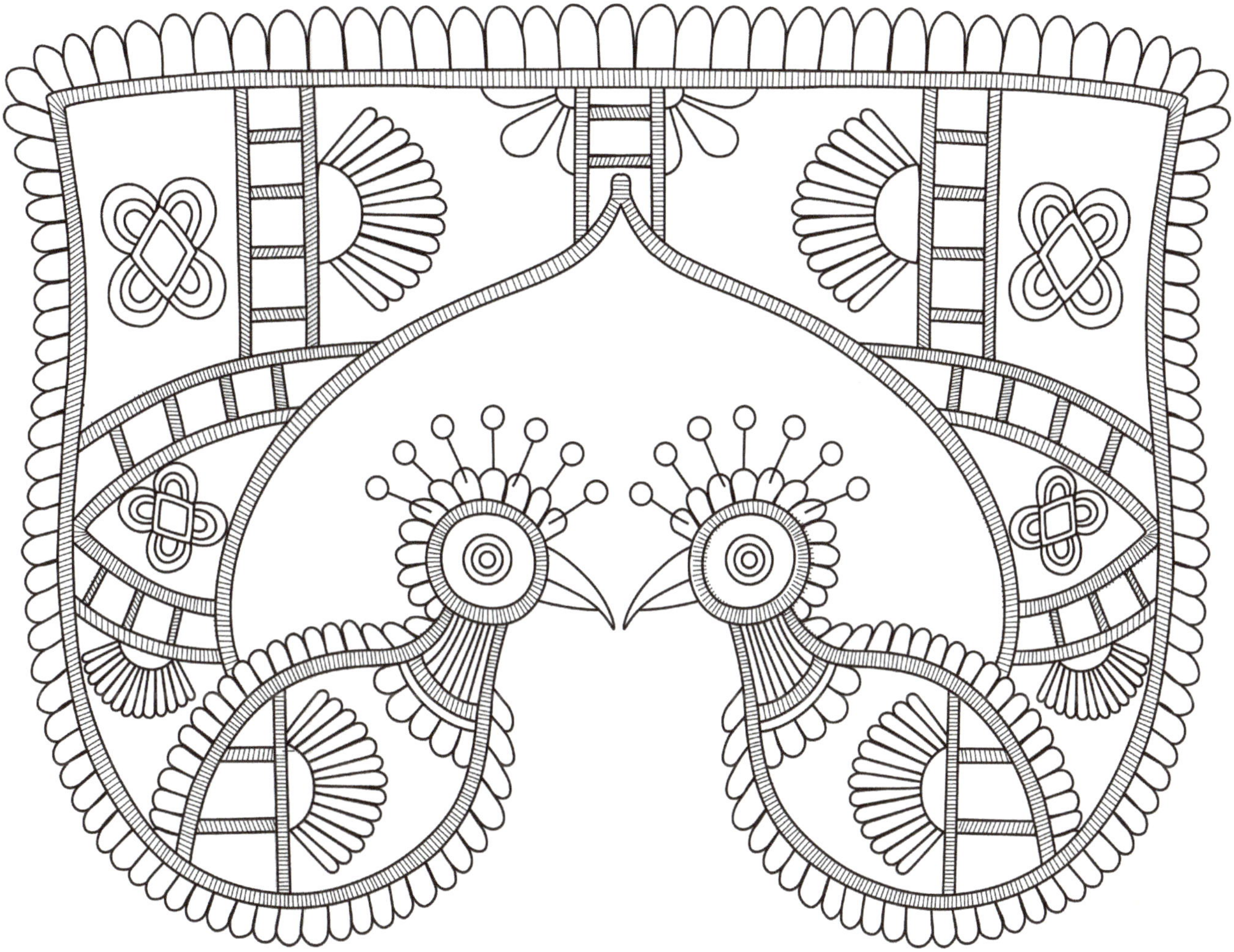

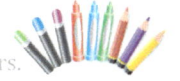

Color the drawing above using your preferred choice of colors.

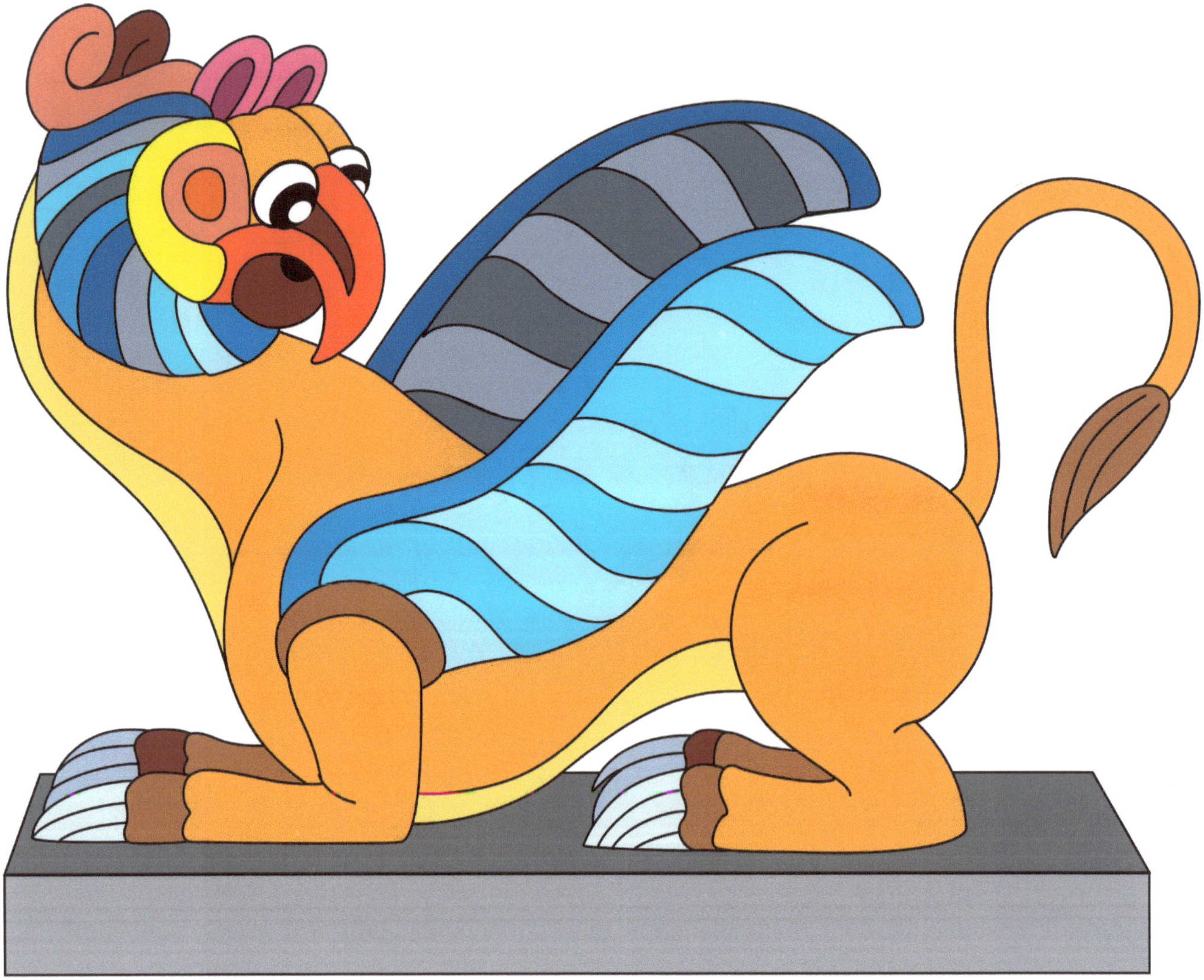

Griffin on the upper portion of a railing post
on the Stupa of Saints, Sanchi. The second half of 2nd Century B.C.E.

12

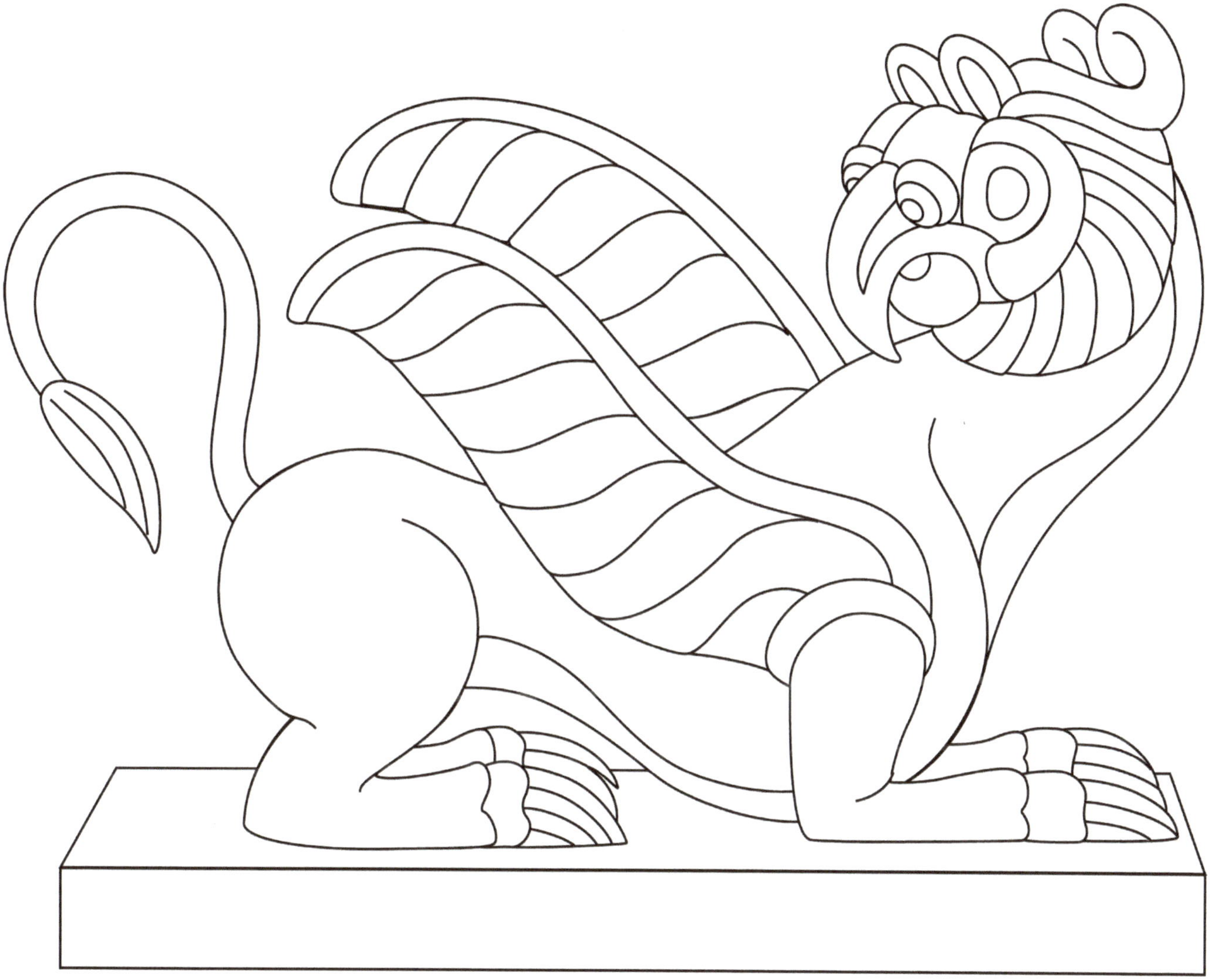

Color the drawing above using your preferred choice of colors.

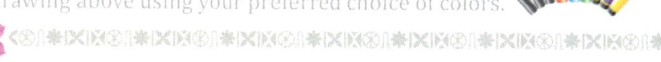

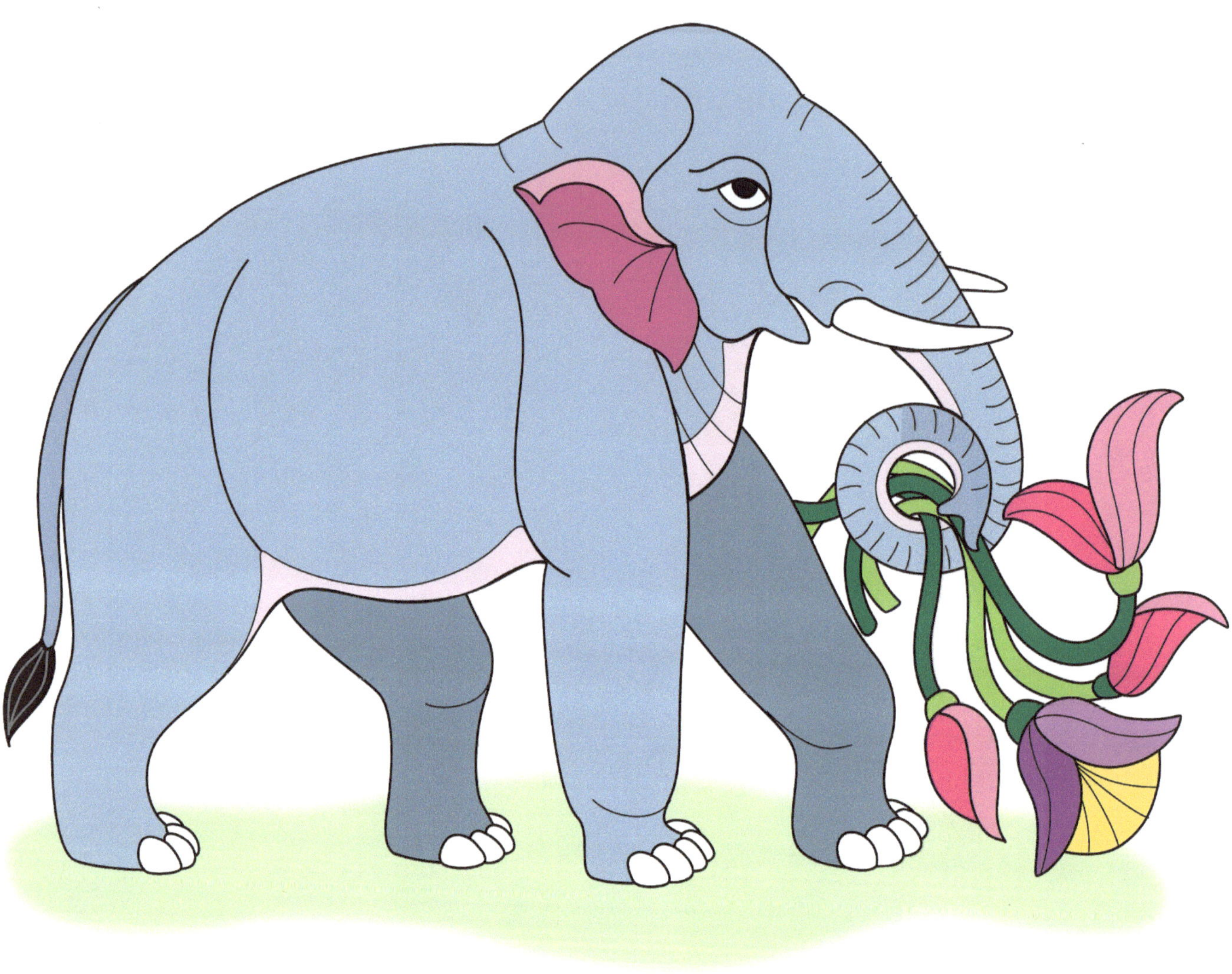

On the carvings of Sanchi Pillar, Sandstone, 1st Century B.C.E.
Flowers, birds and beasts, reflecting the closeness which the Indians
have always felt for the world of nature.

It is only in Indian art we find an intimate relation between the world of
physical beauty and the world of spirit.

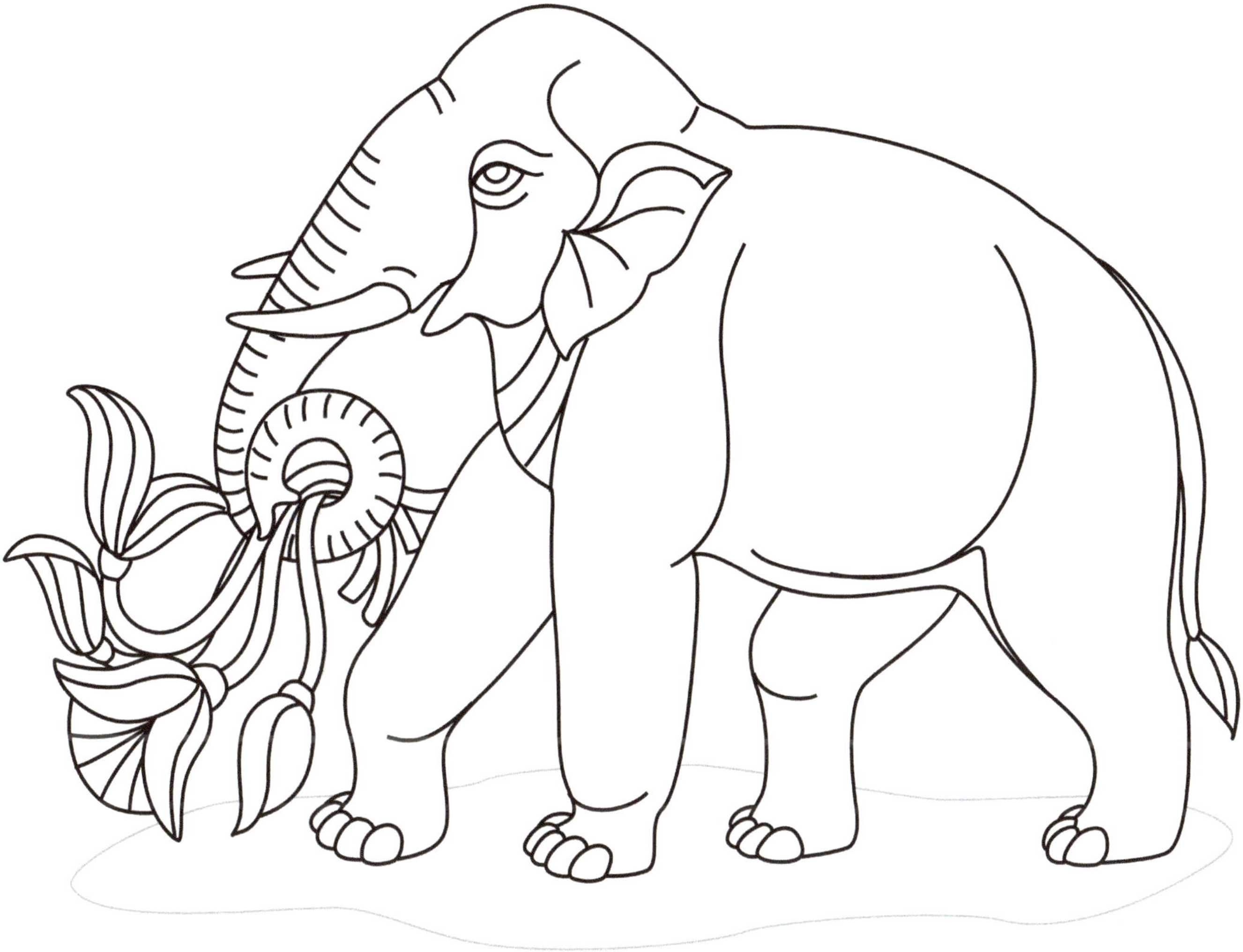

Color the drawing above using your preferred choice of colors.

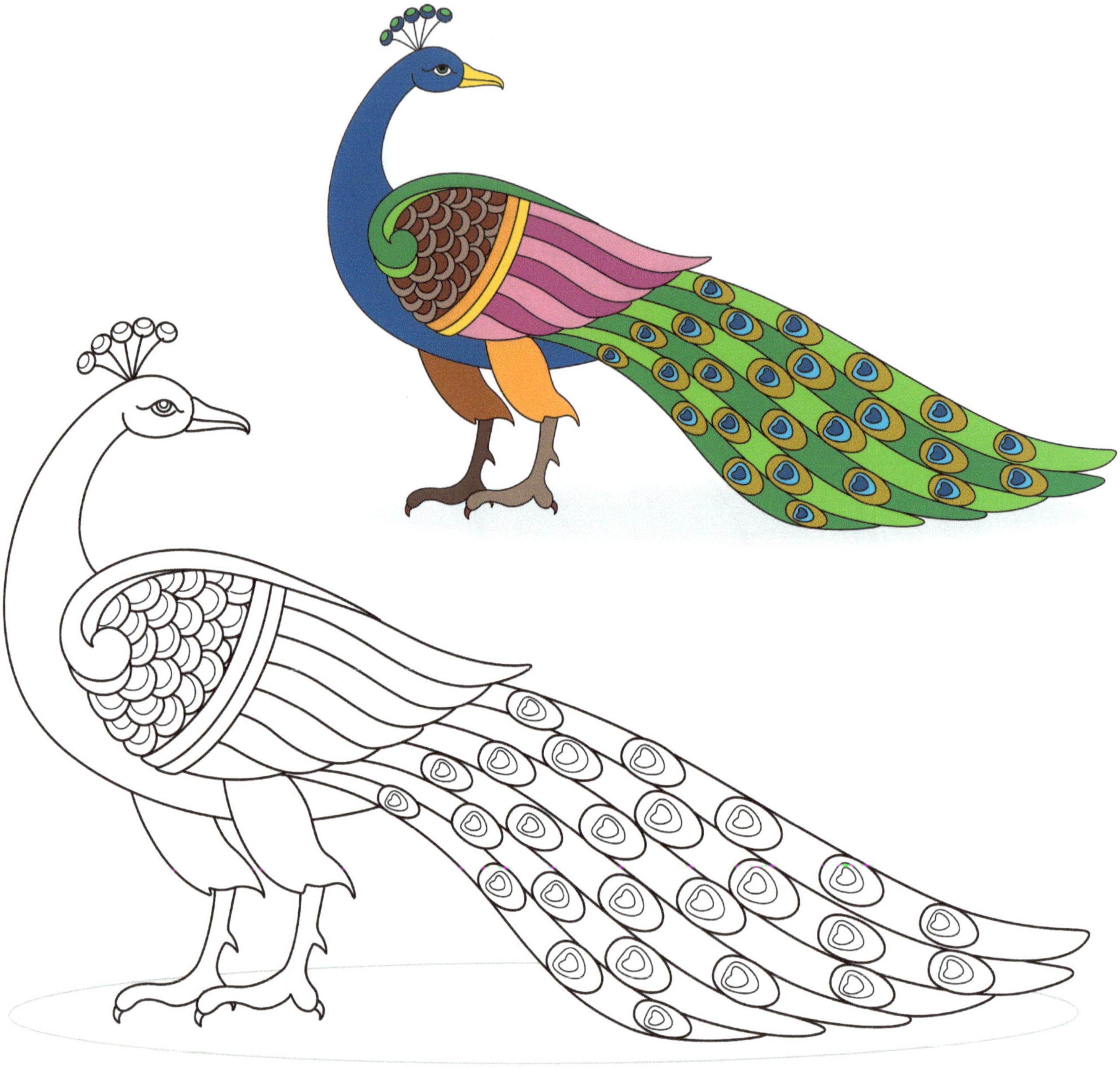

*Facing Pages: Peacock and a mythical creature from the
great Stupa of Sanchi, 1st Century B.C.E.*

Color the drawings above using your preferred choice of colors.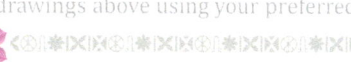

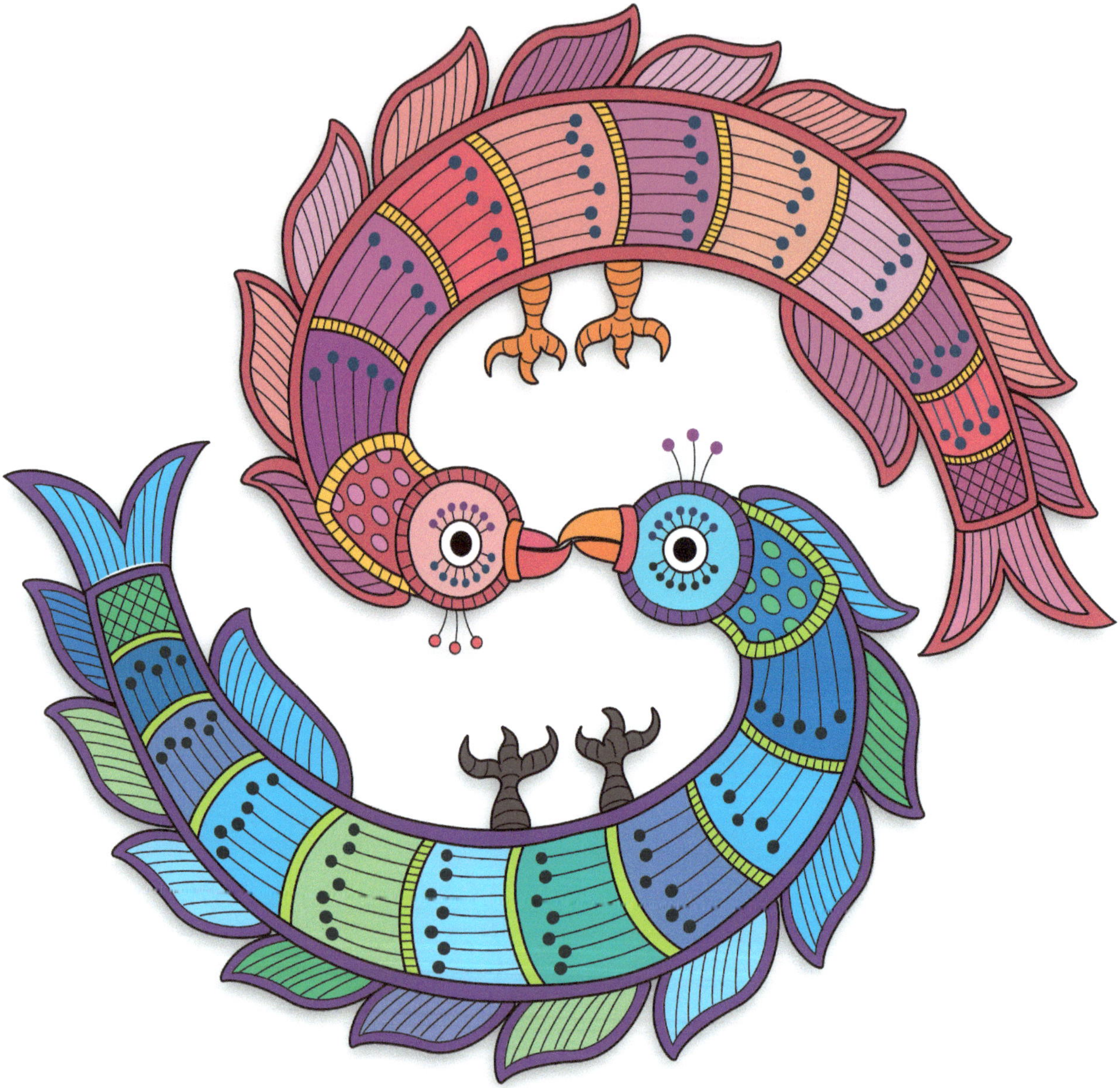

Love birds. Mithila art. Bihar, India.

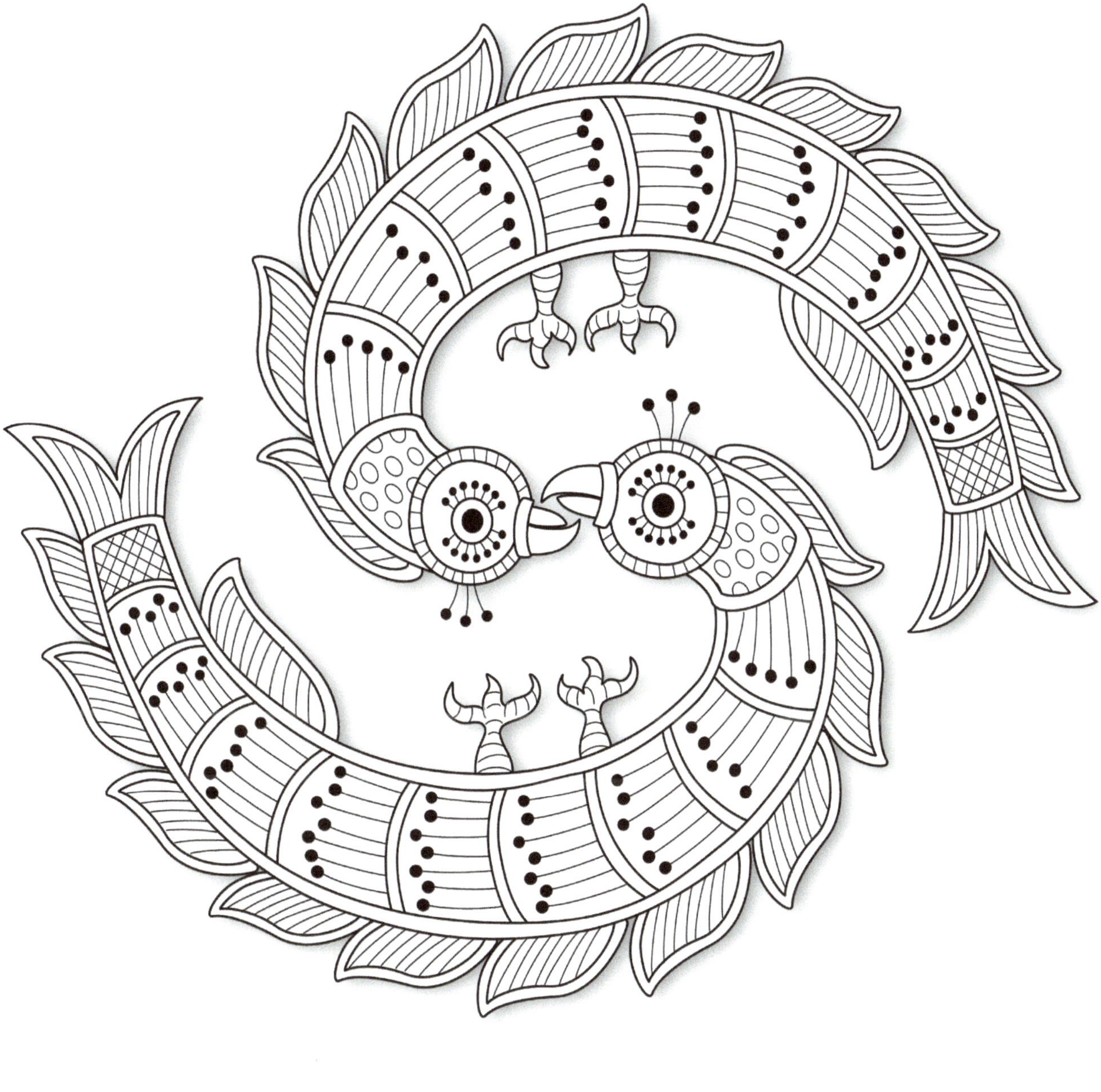

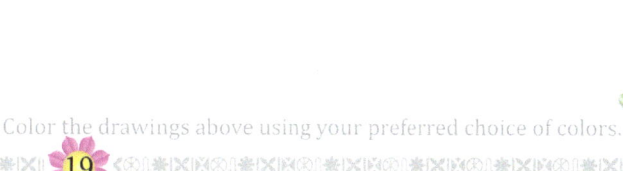

Color the drawings above using your preferred choice of colors.

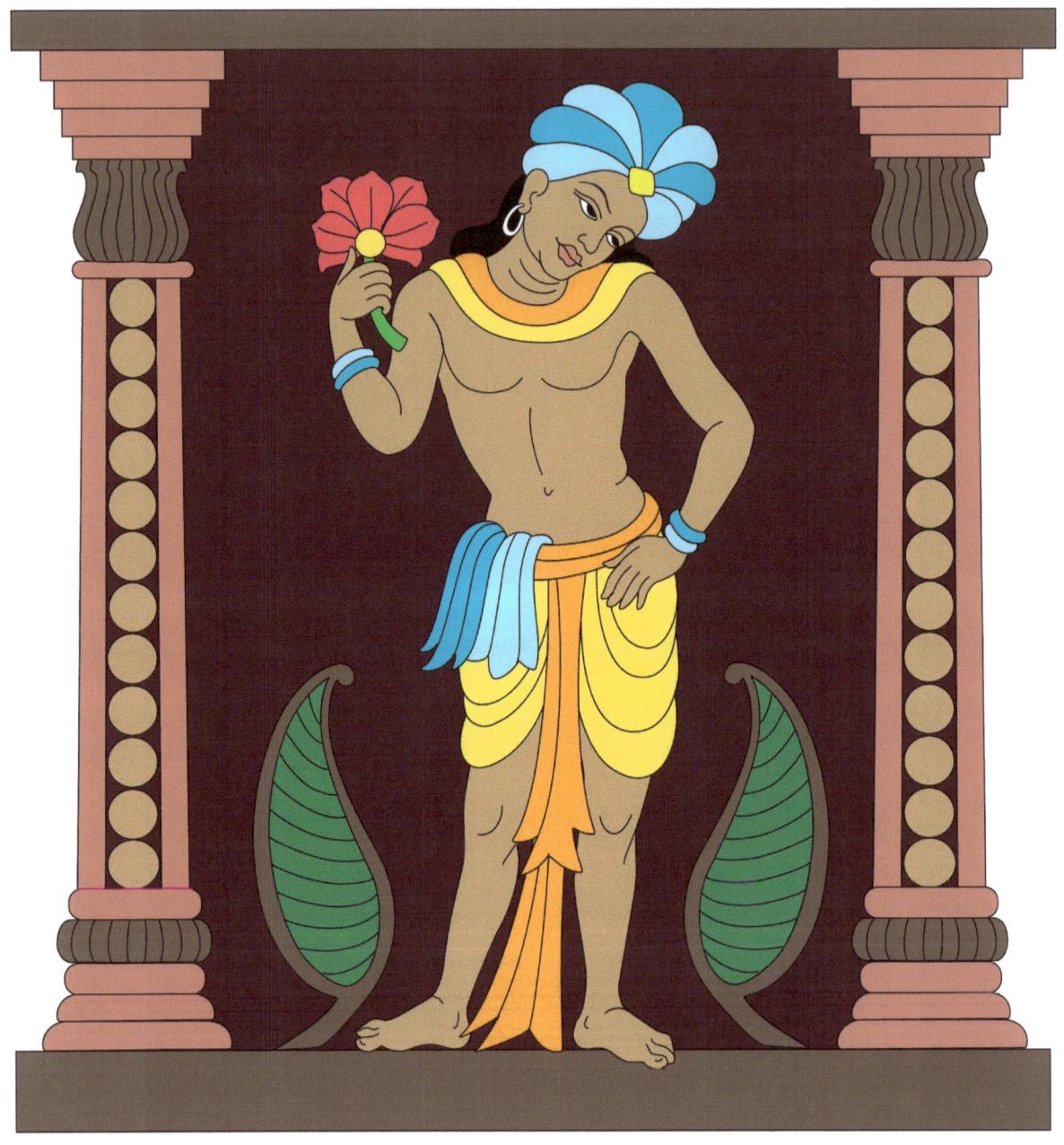

Relief work on marble from Stupa of Amravati. Andhra period, 2nd Century C.E.

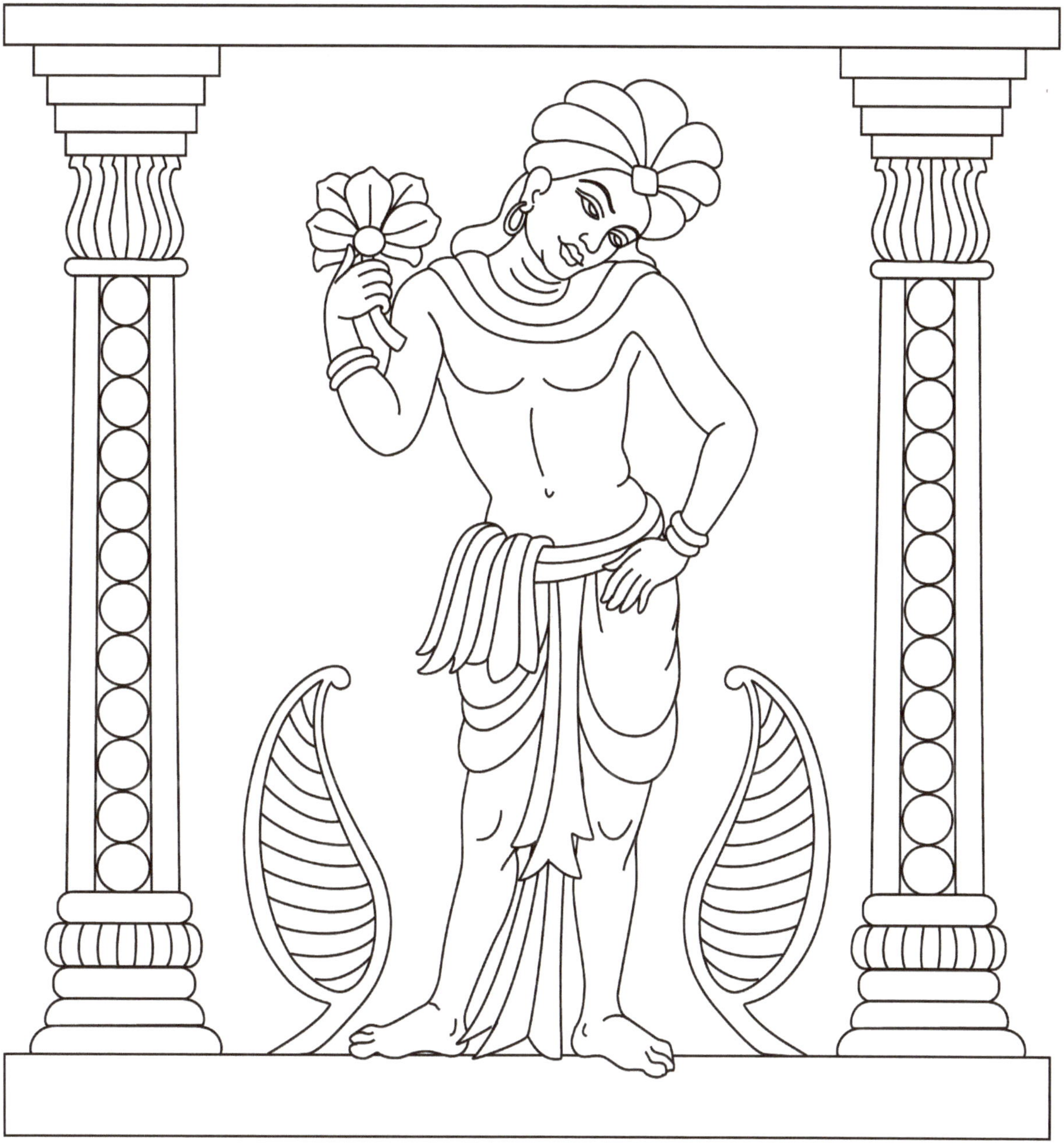

Color the drawing above using your preferred choice of colors.

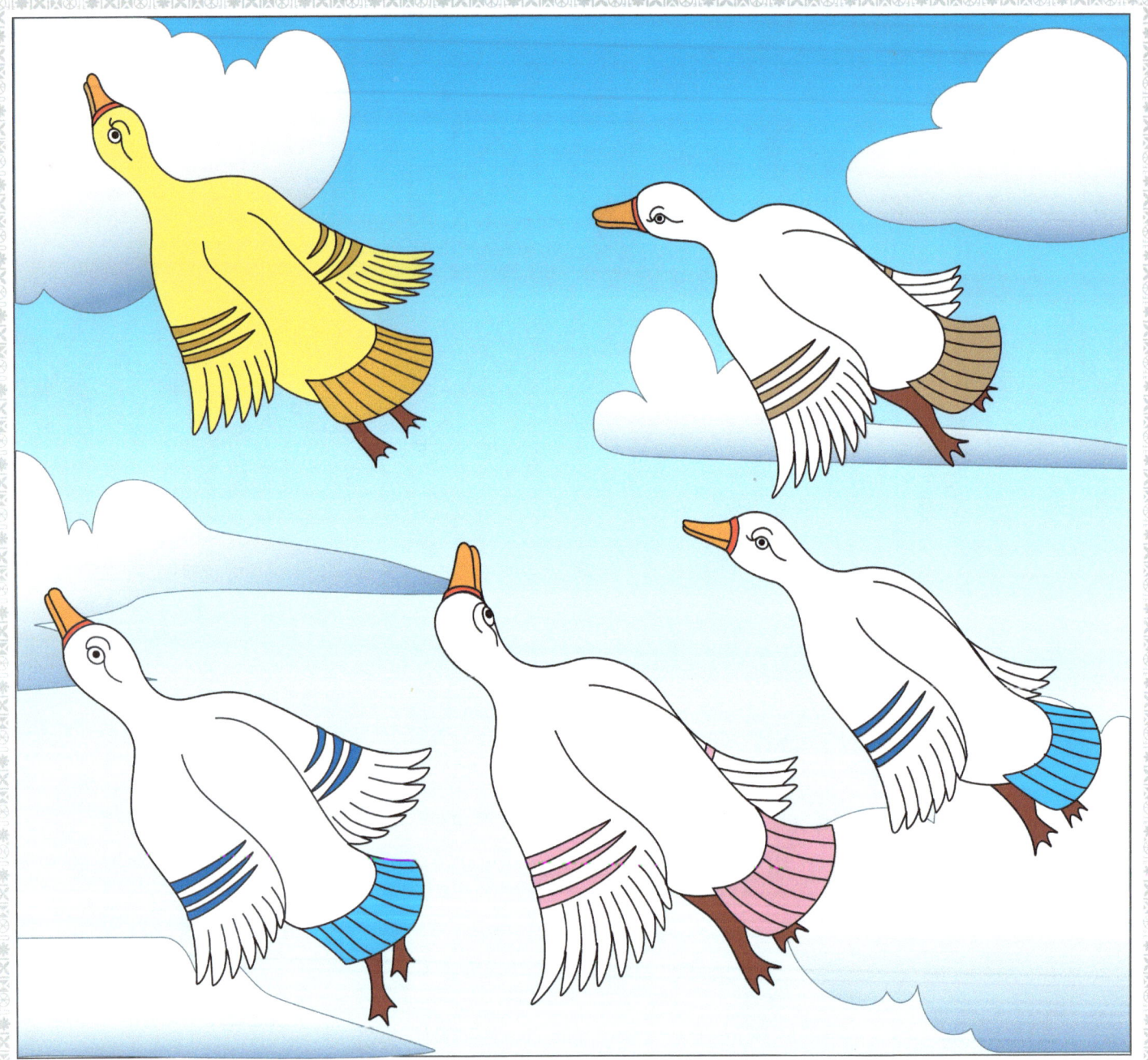

Golden Goose, The King of the Geese from Hamsa Jataka. Ajanta Cave Painting. Middle of 5th Century C.E.

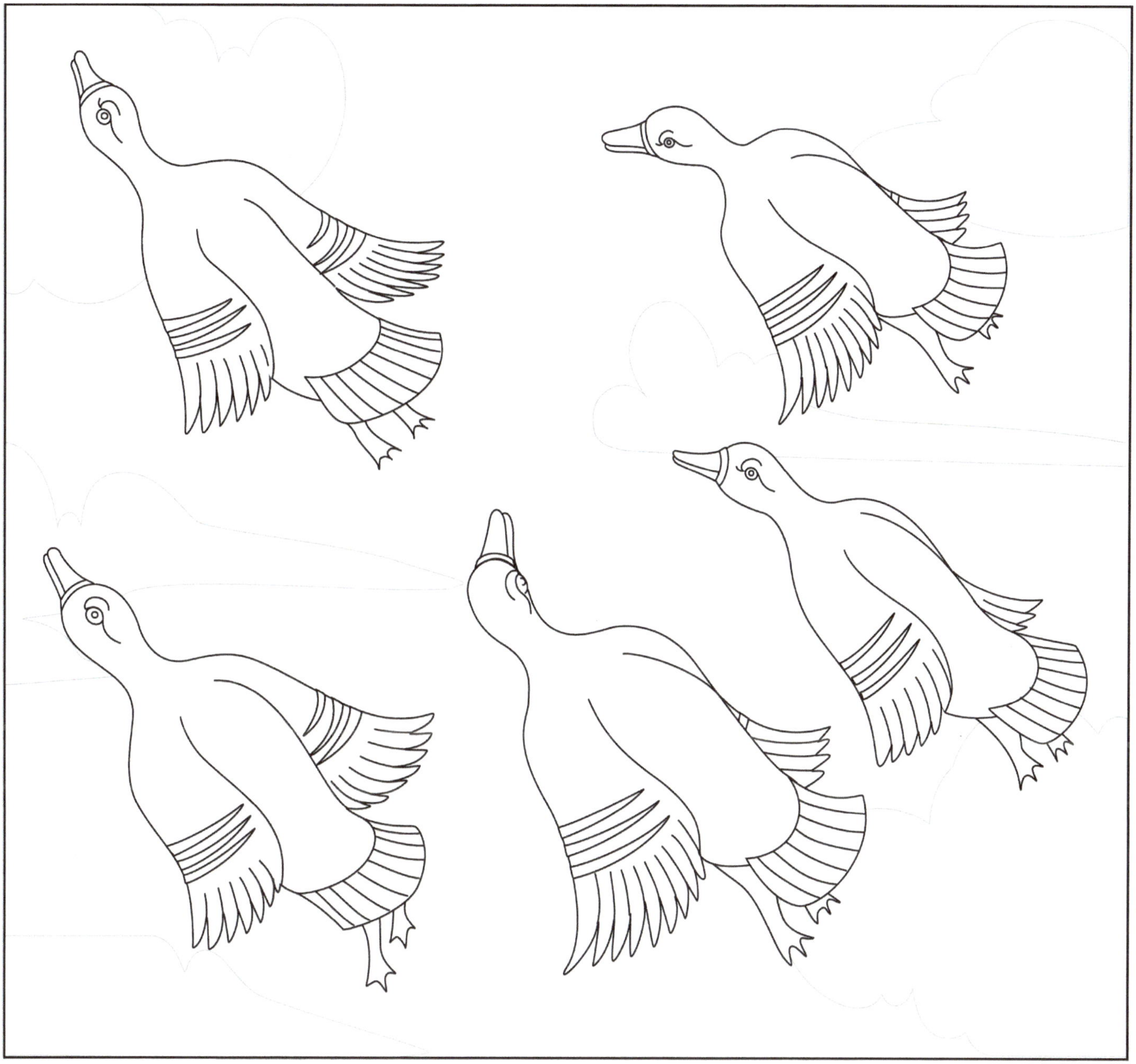

Color the drawing above using your preferred choice of colors.

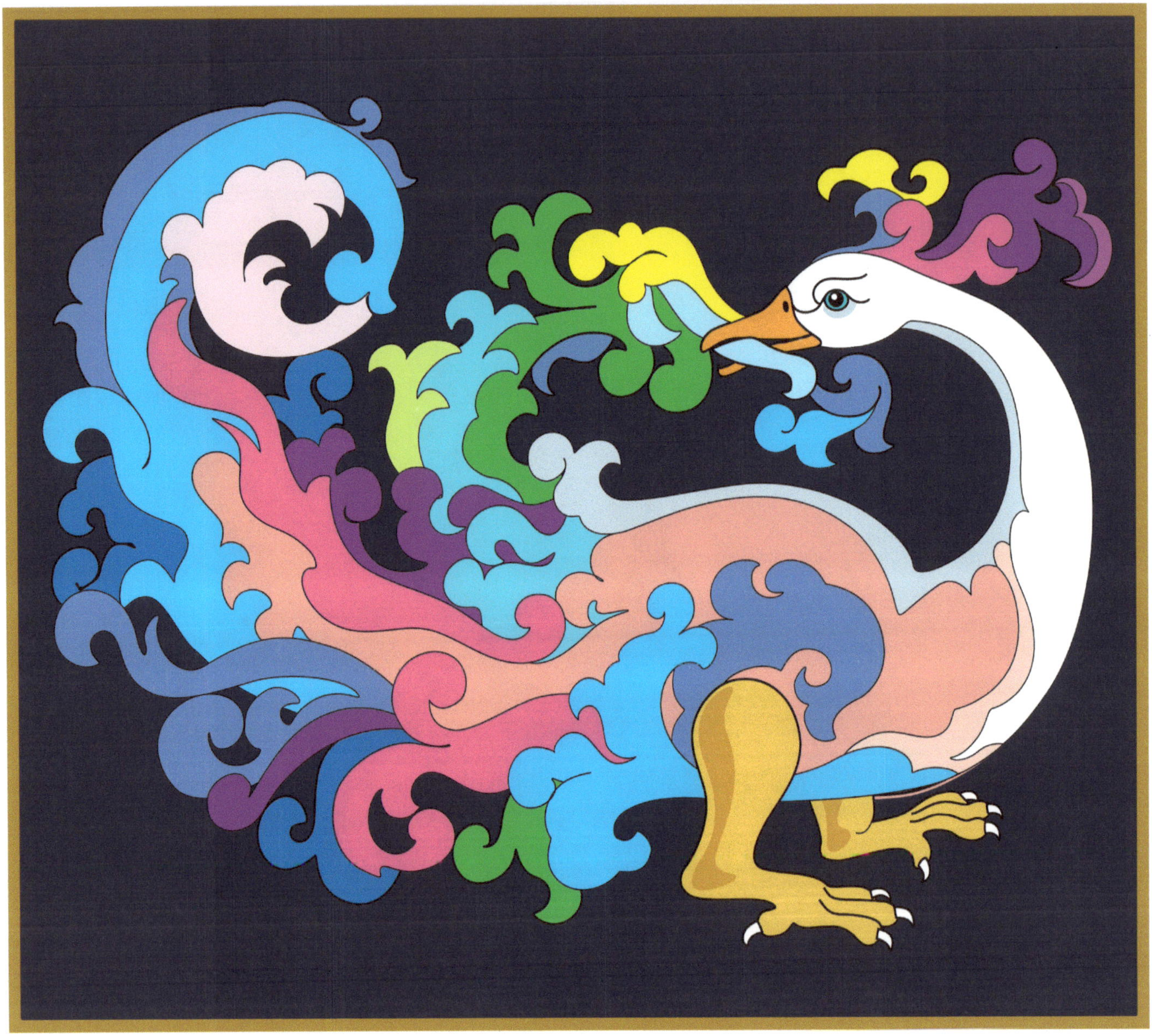

Hamsa, beautiful and stylized relief on
North wall of Virupaksha Temple, Pattadakal. Circa 740 C.E.

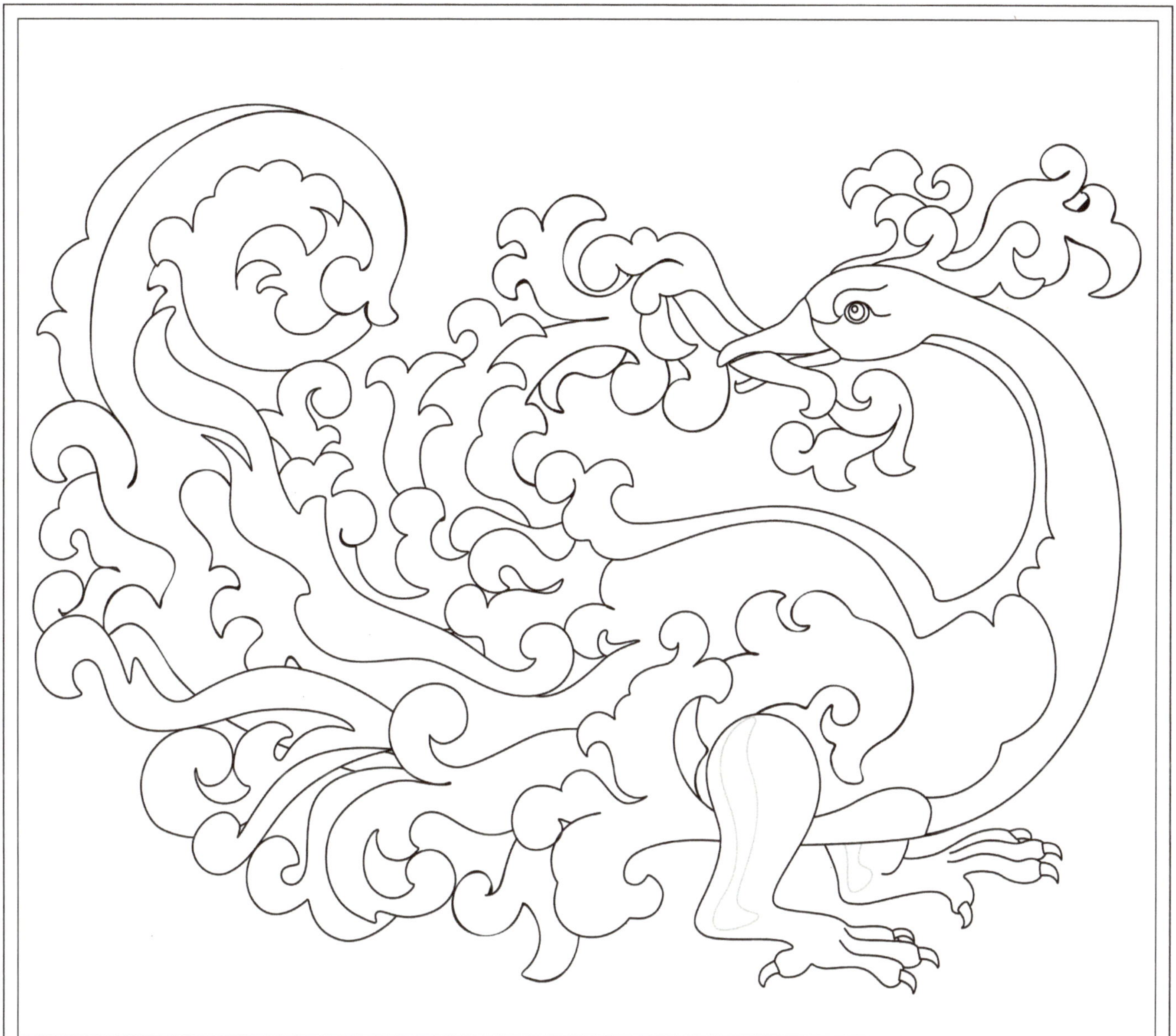

Color the drawing above using your preferred choice of colors.

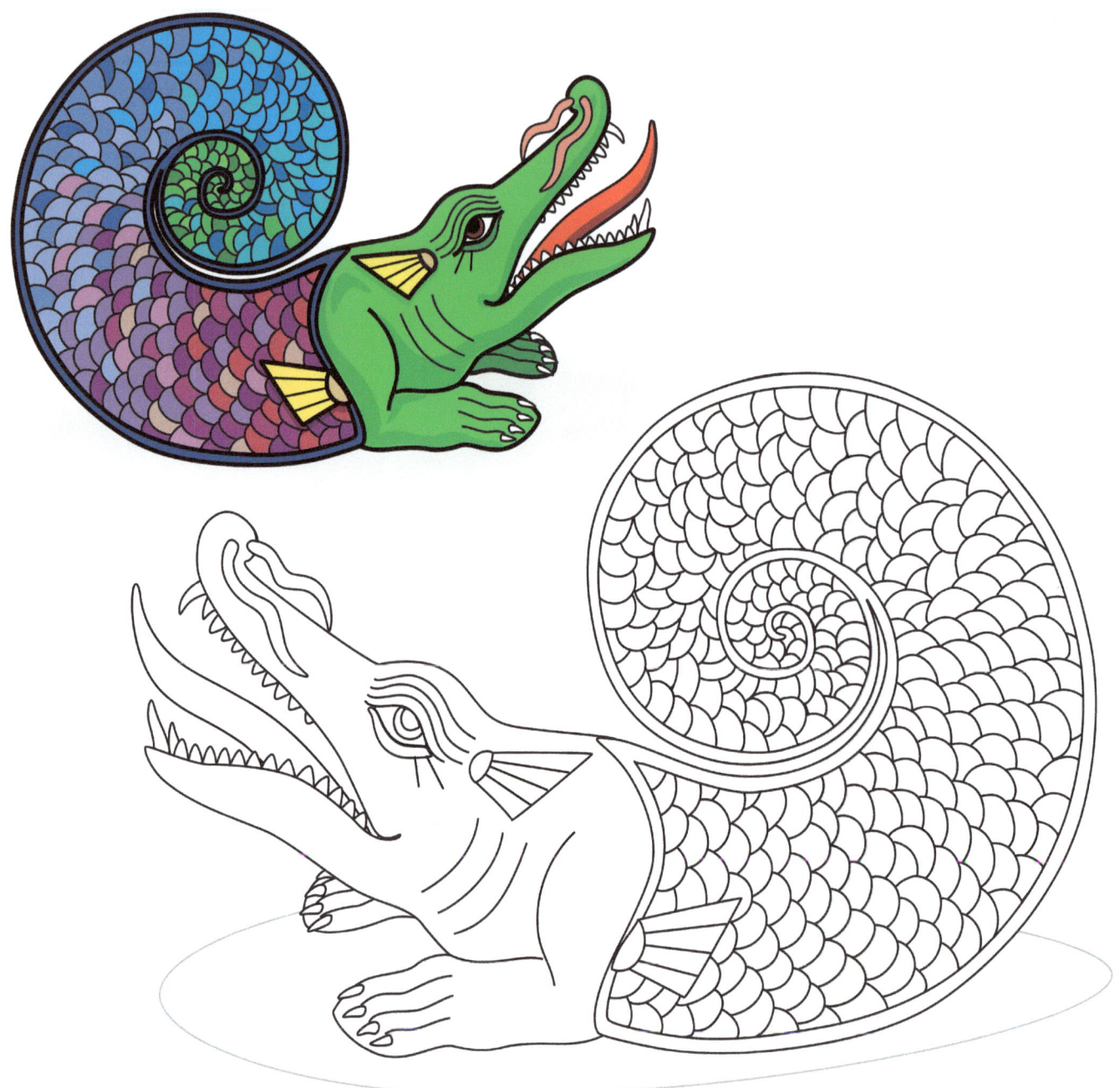

Makara, end of the beam of the gateway of the Stupa of Bharhut. About 100 B.C.E.

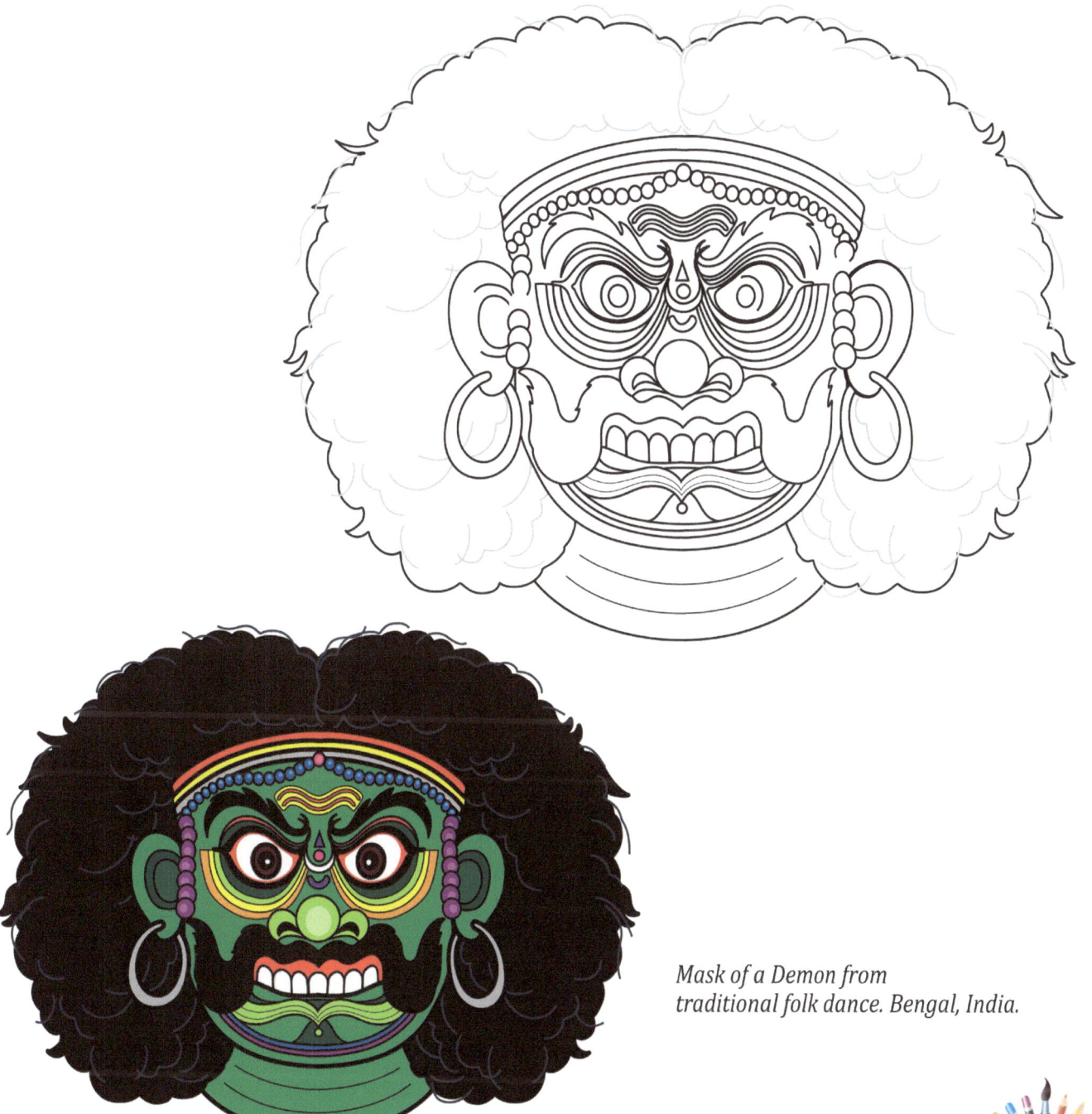

*Mask of a Demon from
traditional folk dance. Bengal, India.*

Color the drawings above using your preferred choice of colors.

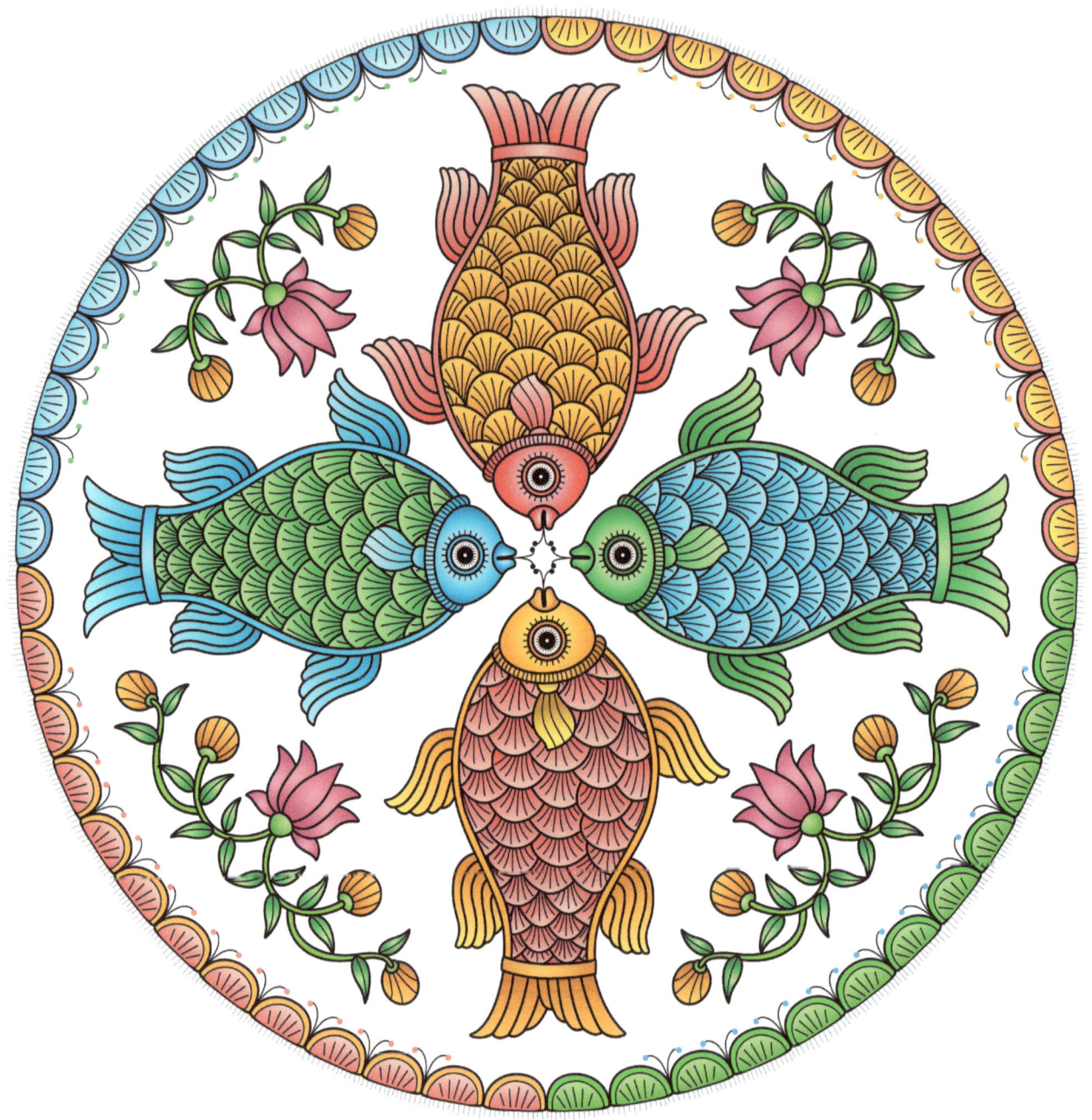

Mithila painting with fish aripana, depicting the cycle of life.

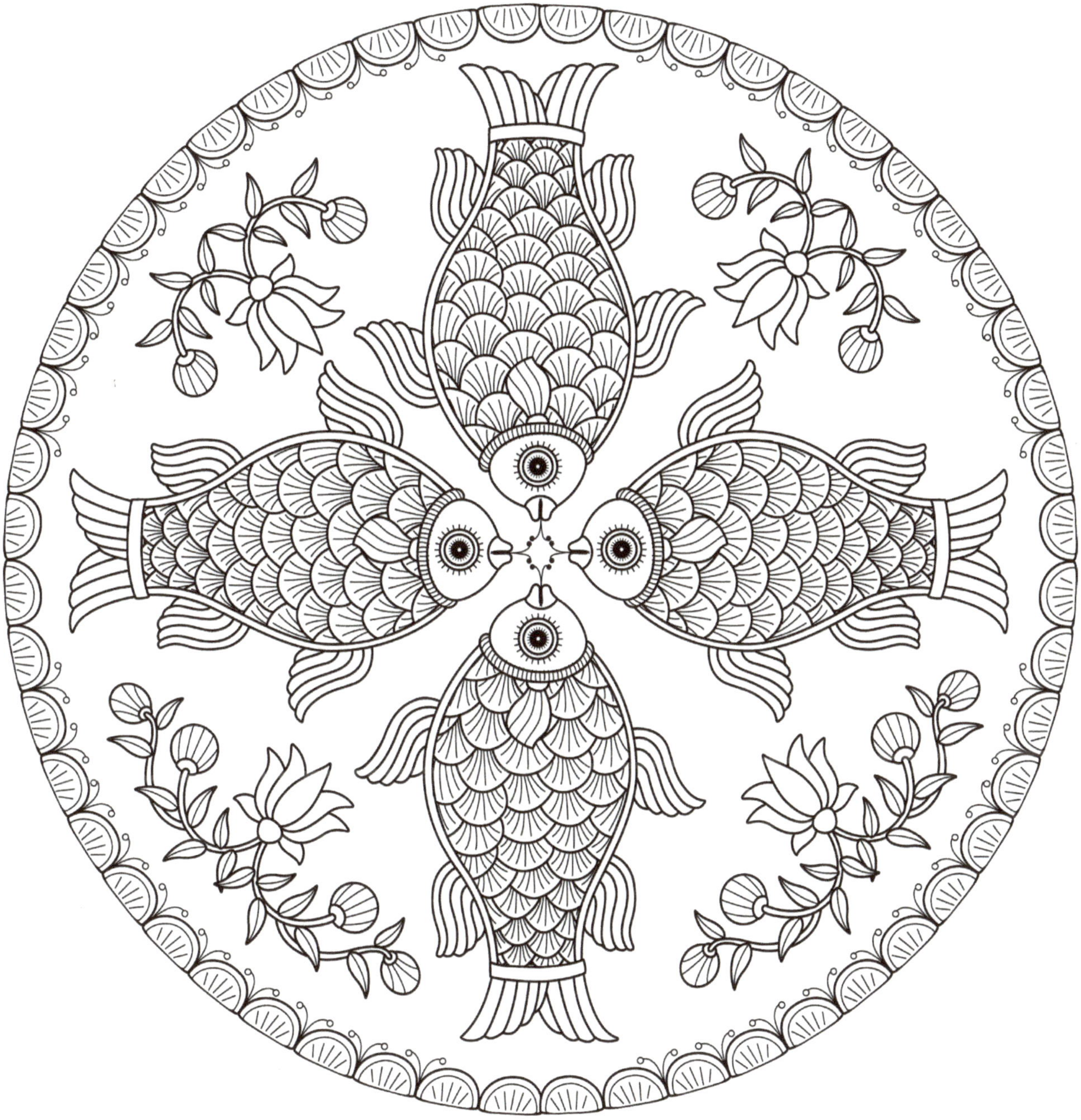

Color the drawing above using your preferred choice of colors.

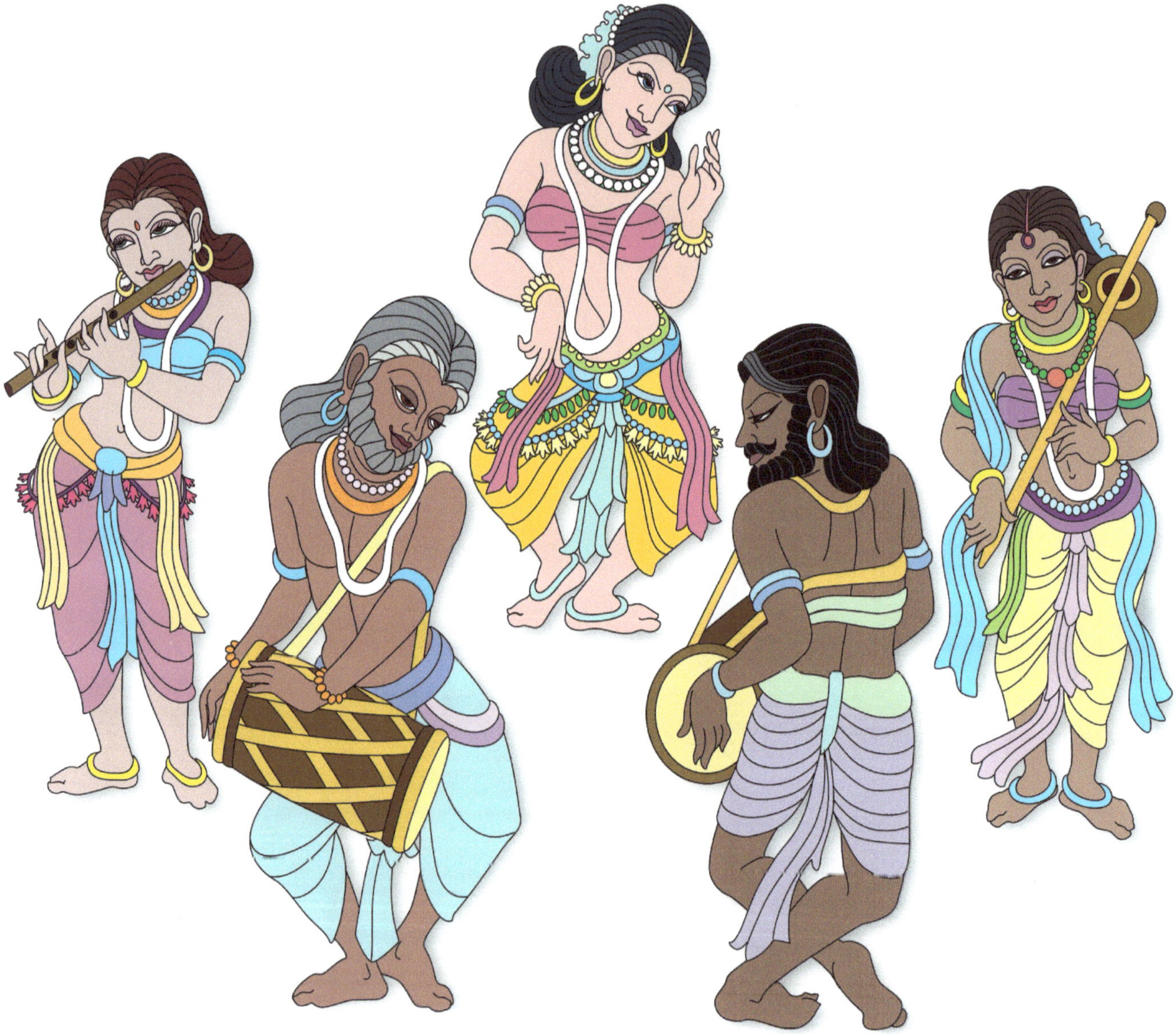

The scene of dance and music, from Purana Mahadeo Harshgiri Temple. Rajasthan. 961 - 973 C.E.

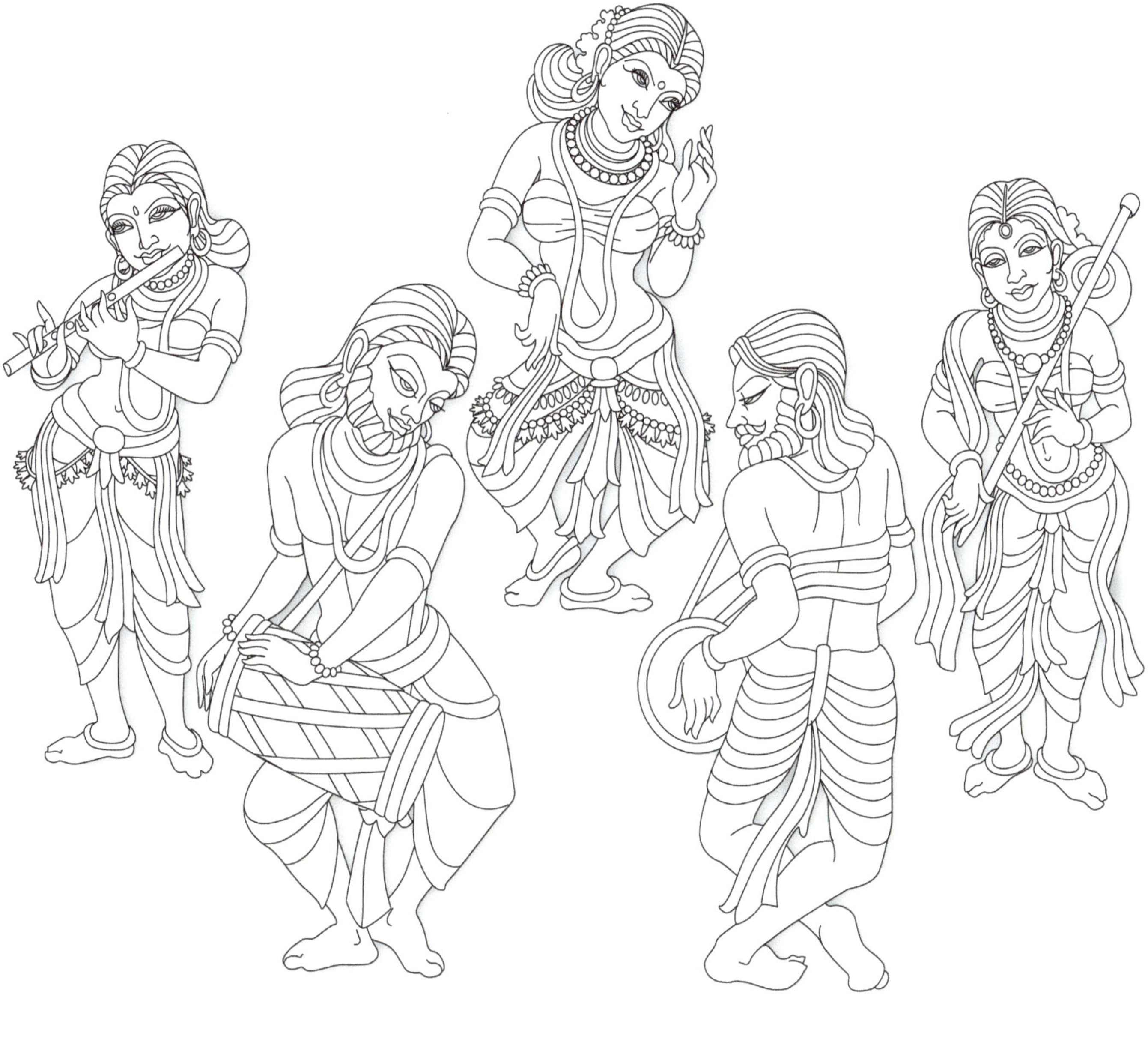

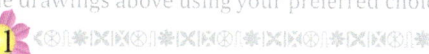

Color the drawings above using your preferred choice of colors.

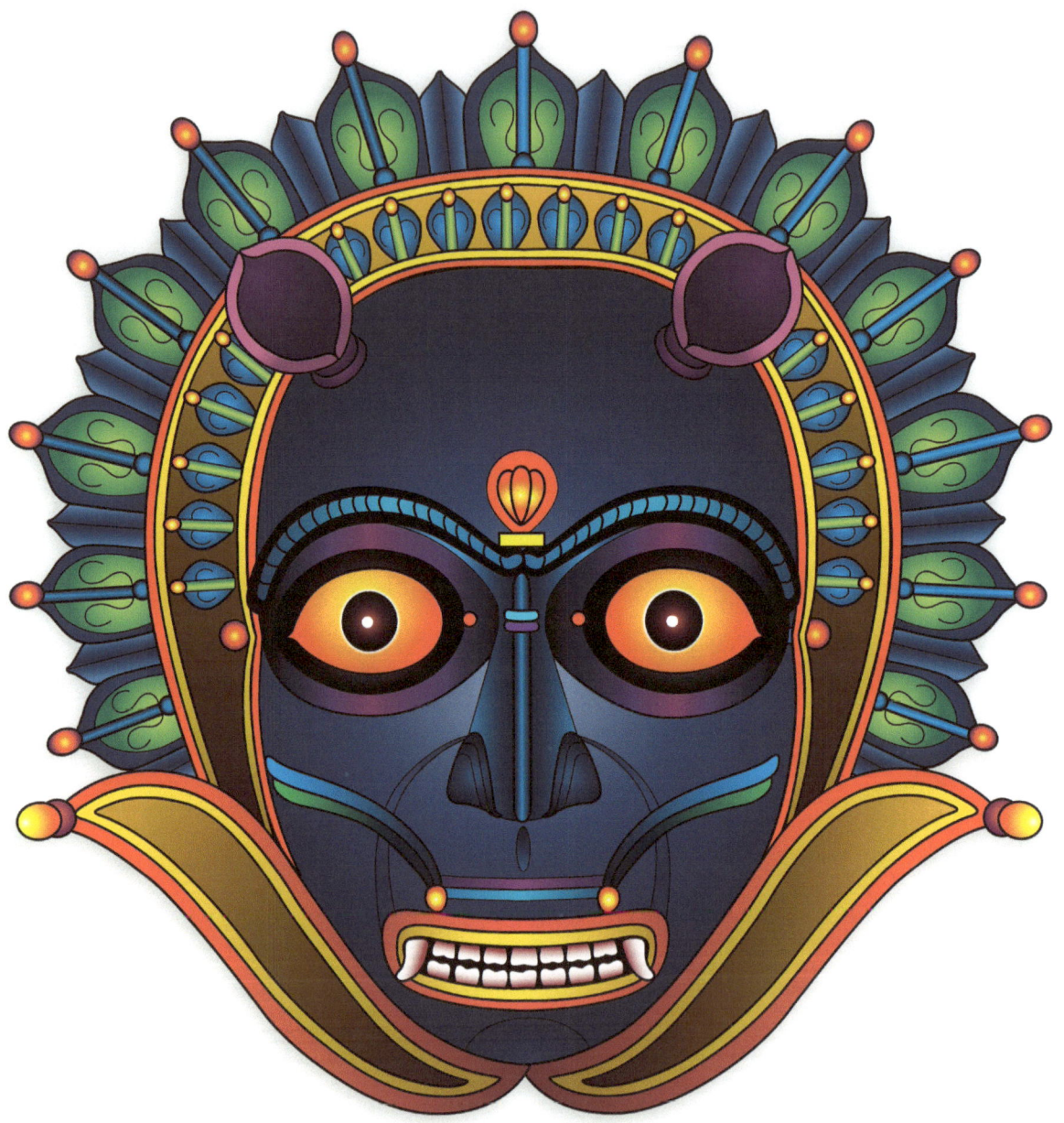

Demon (Bhuta) Mask with feline ears and whiskers, 19th Century bronze from South India.
The mask is worn by dancers during religious festivals. It is believed, the demon comes to inhibit
the body of the dancer and later slain by the mother goddess herself.

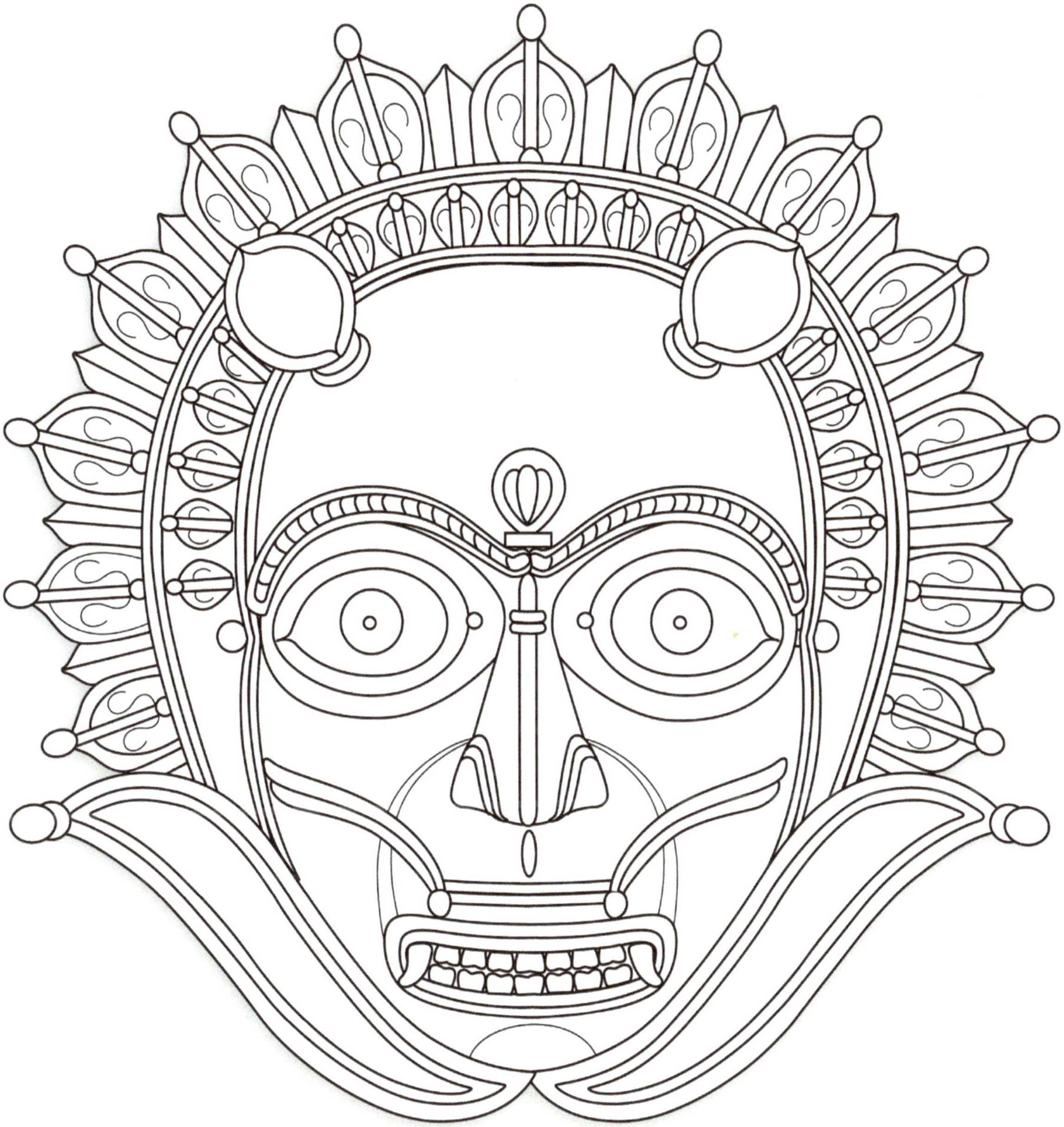

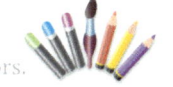

Color the drawing above using your preferred choice of colors.

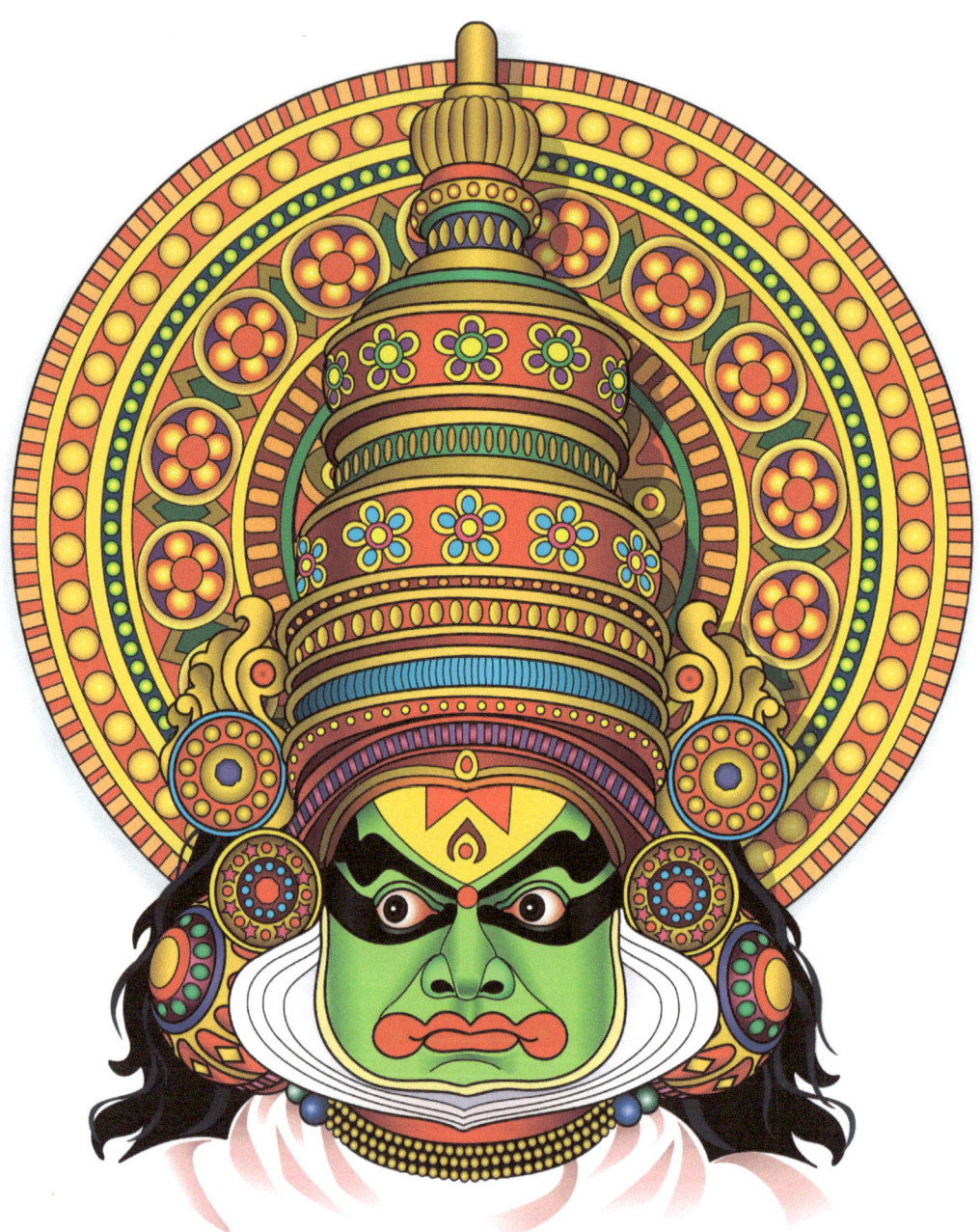

Kathakali performer with makeup and costumes. Kathakali is a stylized
Indian classical dance-drama from the state of Kerala. It dates back to 17th Century C.E.

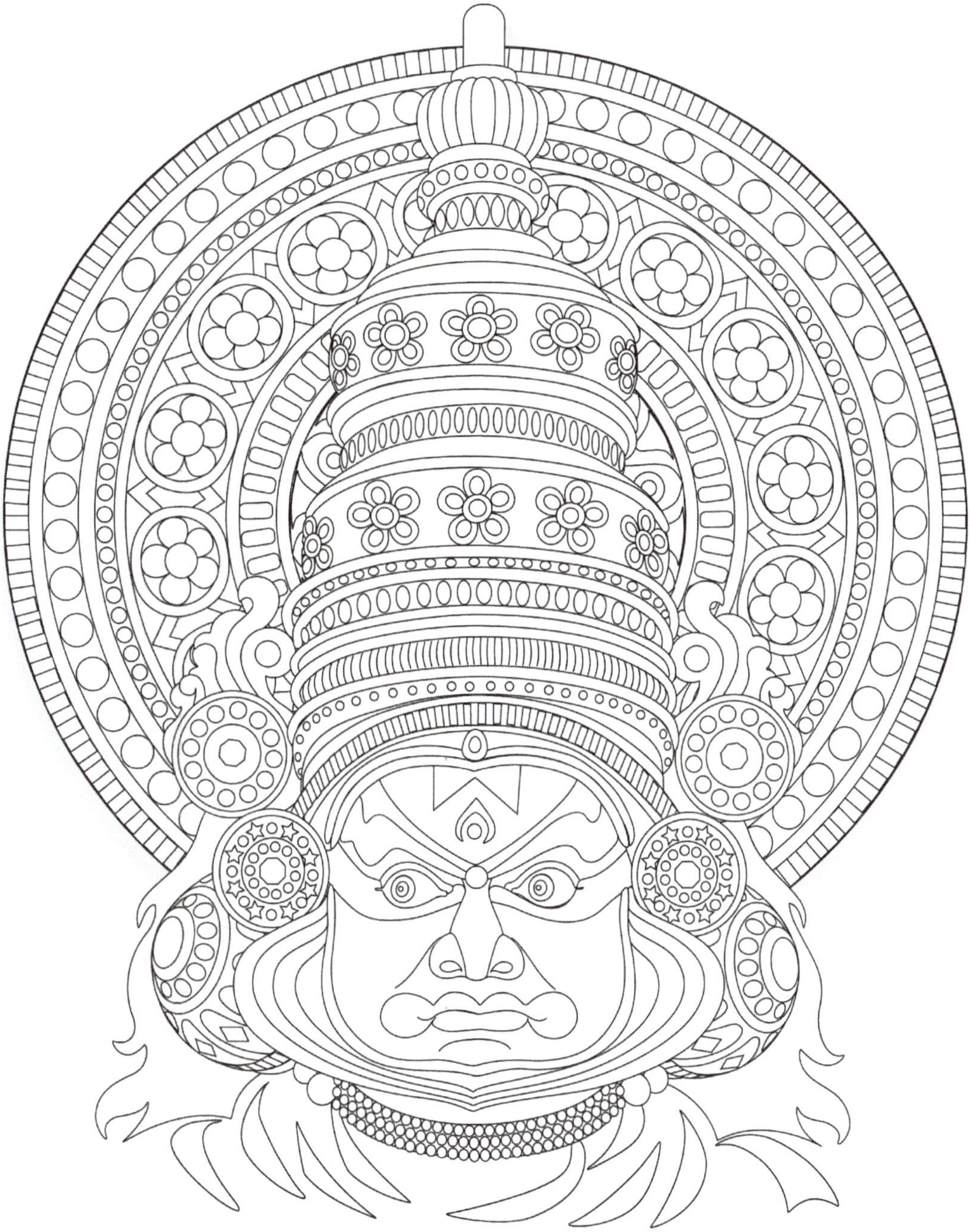

Color the drawing above using your preferred choice of colors.

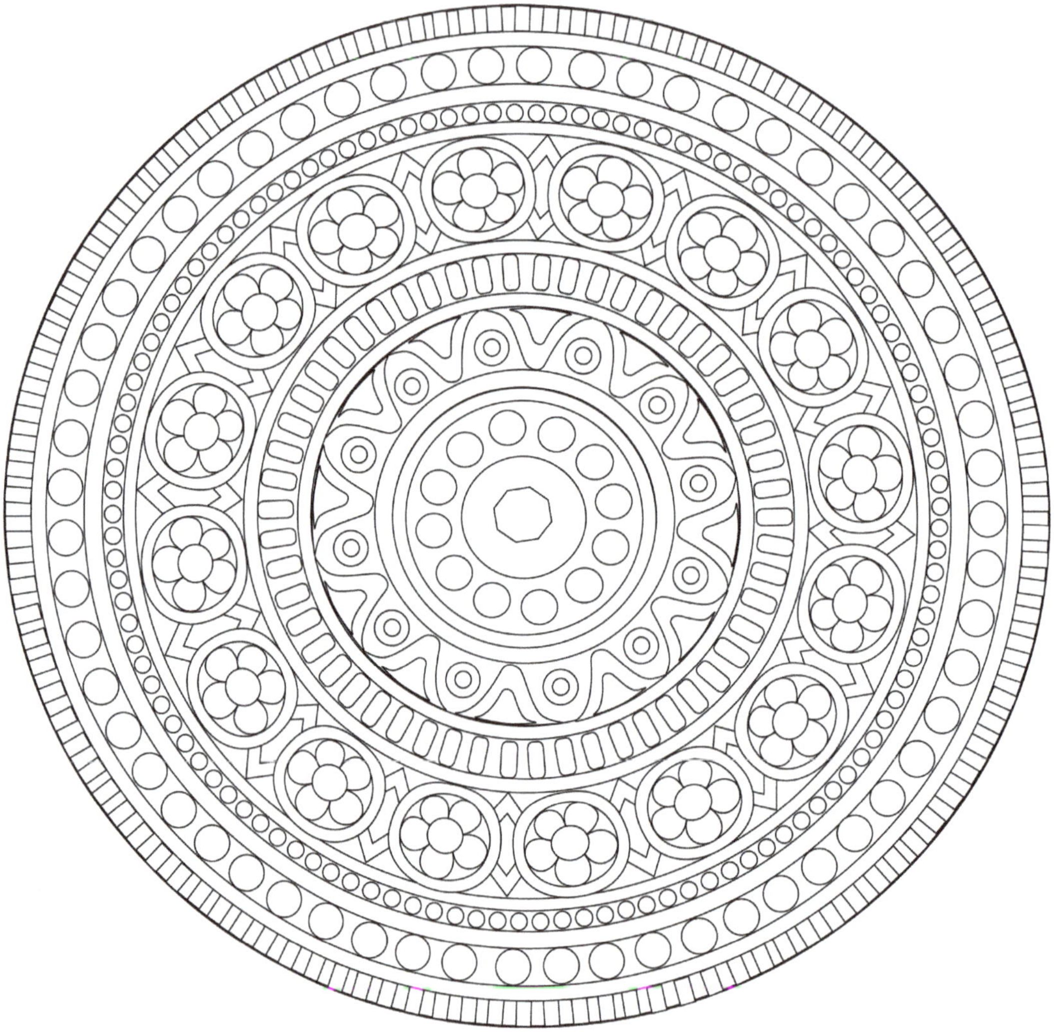

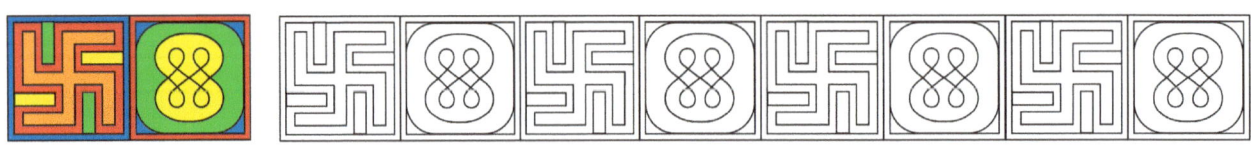

Using these images as examples, create your own piece using the elements found in Indian Art.

Color the drawings above using your preferred choice of colors.

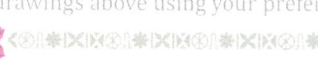

= a synopsis of =
indian art

Indian art is mostly visual art produced on the Indian subcontinent since 4000 B.C.E., and earlier.
Indus Valley Civilization, also known as the Harappan Civilization had matured during 2600 - 1900 B.C.E.
Sculptures made from stone, bronze, and clay in the Indus Valley Civilization had first introduced
the distinct artistic elements that later became permanent characteristics of Indian art.
Terracotta was the most treasured material for Indus sculptors.

The Stupas at Amravati, Sanchi, Bharhut, and others display the wealth of stone carvings.
The themes that united the Stupas together are scenes from the life of Buddha. At the Sanchi Gates,
there are depictions of warriors on horses, royal processions, traders, caravans, and merchants,
farmers with produce and animals, and so forth. Indian temples sculpted images of musicians,
acrobats, romantic couples, and a variety of deities. Hindu sculptures were naturalistic in all
and mainly focused on creating humans, animals, vegetables, and other forms of life. Indian color,
while sometimes shining with the lovely orange-amber light in the Ajanta cave paintings,
is essentially delicate, and its use in decoration varies with each art.

Paintings in India have a very tradition with ancient texts outlining theories of color and aesthetics.
Common households used to paint doorways and facades. Cave paintings from Ajanta, Bagh, and
Sittanavasal, as well as temple paintings, confirm the love of naturalizing the human form and
nature in a manner that is aesthetically pleasing and as an embellishment. Miniature paintings on paper
developed quickly in the late 16th Century from the combined influences of the existing Indian
tradition and the imported Persian style by the Mughals. In many of the Indian Miniature paintings,
the emphasis is placed on mood or atmosphere through the bold use of color and deliberate flattering of
three-dimensional textures. The artists succeeded in bringing out hidden nuances that simply
would not be possible any other way. In both the Mewer and in Kangra paintings,
scenes of idyllic nature were created to convey joy and romance.

Folk and tribal art in India took on different manifestations through a varied media such as; pottery,
painting, metal work, paper art, weaving, jewelry, toys, and masks. All these play a great role in the
populations both daily and ritual life. The folk spirit played an important part in the development
of Indian art and in the overall perception of the indigenous people of India.

OTHER TITLES IN THIS SERIES

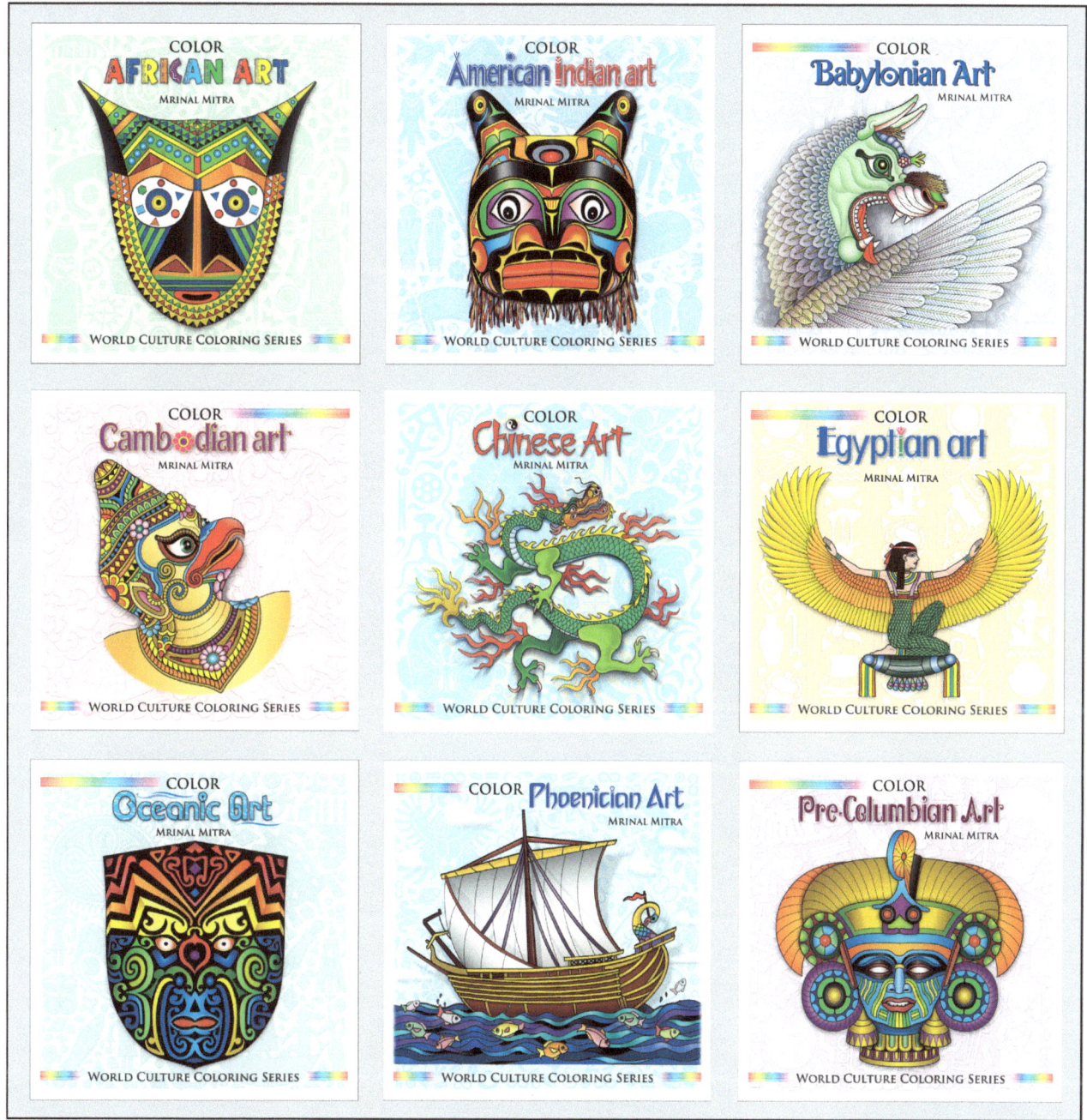

Acknowledgement

First and foremost, this series would not be possible without the number of great historical art found within the different cultural regions around the world.

In addition, we would like to acknowledge the variety of publishing's from all over the world for allowing us to learn about their fascinating ancestral art and culture. With this provided knowledge, we have hoped to have represented the art as splendidly as you have supplied it.

About the Author

Mrinal Mitra has earned a number of prestigious awards, both Indian and International, and received honors for his outstanding illustrations. Some of his recognitions include; The Noma Concours Award, Japan (twice), Illustrators Award, and Children's Choice Award, India, and honors from German Television "Transtel", BRNO- CSSR, TIBI- Iran, and UNICEF, New York.

Many of his talented artworks have been exhibited in several different countries such as; India, Japan, Italy, Czech Republic, Iran, and New Zealand. Mitra has authored, designed and illustrated trade and educational children's books for many Indian as well as Multinational Book Publishers around the globe.

Copyright: Mrinal Mitra, 2014

Printed by CreateSpace, An Amazon.com. Company
Available from Amazon.com, CreateSpace.com, and other retail outlets

For further inquiry please contact Mrinal Mitra at: mitra_mrinal@hotmail.com